D. Allen

YOGA DICTIONARY

MIDCENTURY
REFERENCE LIBRARY

DAGOBERT D. RUNES, Ph.D., *General Editor*

AVAILABLE

Beethoven Encyclopedia
Dictionary of American Grammar
and Usage
Dictionary of American Maxims
Dictionary of American Proverbs
Dictionary of Ancient History
Dictionary of Arts and Crafts
Dictionary of the Arts
Dictionary of Civics and Government
Dictionary of European History
Dictionary of Etiquette
Dictionary of Foreign Words
and Phrases
Dictionary of Forgotten Words
Dictionary of Last Words
Dictionary of Latin Literature
Dictionary of Linguistics
Dictionary of Mysticism
Dictionary of Mythology
Dictionary of Pastoral Psychology
Dictionary of Philosophy
Dictionary of Psychoanalysis
Dictionary of Science and Technology

Dictionary of Sociology
Dictionary of Word Origins
Dictionary of World Literature
Encyclopedia of Aberrations
Encyclopedia of the Arts
Encyclopedia of Atomic Energy
Encyclopedia of Criminology
Encyclopedia of Literature
Encyclopedia of Psychology
Encyclopedia of Religion
Encyclopedia of Substitutes and
Synthetics
Encyclopedia of Vocational Guidance
Illustrated Technical Dictionary
Labor Dictionary
Liberal Arts Dictionary
Military and Naval Dictionary
New Dictionary of American History
New Dictionary of Psychology
Protestant Dictionary
Slavonic Encyclopedia
Theatre Dictionary
Tobacco Dictionary

FORTHCOMING

Buddhist Dictionary
Dictionary of American Folklore
Dictionary of the American Indian
Dictionary of the American Language
Dictionary of American Literature
Dictionary of American Men and Places
Dictionary of American Names
Dictionary of American Superstitions
Dictionary of American Synonyms
Dictionary of Anthropology
Dictionary of Astronomy
Dictionary of Dietetics
Dictionary of Discoveries and Inventions
Dictionary of Earth Sciences
Dictionary of Explorations
Dictionary of French Literature
Dictionary of Geography

Dictionary of German Literature
Dictionary of Hebrew Literature
Dictionary of Law
Dictionary of Magic
Dictionary of Mechanics
Dictionary of New Words
Dictionary of Poetics
Dictionary of the Renaissance
Dictionary of Russian Literature
Dictionary of Science
Dictionary of Social Science
Dictionary of Spanish Literature
Encyclopedia of Morals
Personnel Dictionary
Teachers' Dictionary
Writers' Dictionary

PHILOSOPHICAL LIBRARY, INC.
Publishers

15 E. 40th Street   New York 16, N. Y.

YOGA DICTIONARY

By ERNEST WOOD
Author of GREAT SYSTEMS OF YOGA

PHILOSOPHICAL LIBRARY
New York

Printed in the United States of America

PREFACE

In presenting a dictionary of yoga to the western world, I wish to say that all my technical material and terminology has been taken direct from ancient works in the original Sanskrit language, and particularly from the famous *Sūtras* of Patanjali and the writings of Shankarāchārya with regard to *rāja-yoga* and *jnāna-yoga,* (the yogas of will and knowledge), from the *Bhagavad Gītā* with regard to *karma-yoga* and *buddhi-yoga* (the wisdom and love yogas), and from numerous works such as the *Hatha-yoga Pradīpikā,* the *Gheranda Samhitā,* the *Shiva Samhitā* and many numerous minor Upanishads etc. with regard to *hatha-yoga, laya-yoga* and *mantra-yoga.* As to *bhakti-yoga*—it comes into all the yogas, and all of these also overlap one another. My explanations are for the most part the result of my own experience and much contact with many yogīs in India.

As regards my references to Buddhism Zen and the Sufis, I am very much indebted to various modern works and translations into English. To a large extent the psychology and practices are the same in all systems, except where I have specially noted otherwise under the specific items concerned.

In India, where most of the forms of yoga originally arose, and where it still flourishes and is respected by almost the entire population, we find that it is inextricably bound up with religion. The very word yoga, meaning union, is the same word as religion, which means union—in both cases "with the divine"—or the superhuman—being implied. But along with the word yoga there is always practicability. "Now that we have religion, or religious knowledge, what are we going to do about it?" is a typical question in India as elsewhere, for those people are very energetic and practical in such matters. Really, one may say incidentally, they are so also in material matters, when not too much discouraged, as the old history of India shows, for in older times in all the fields of the industrial arts, especially in the making of carpets and cloths, pottery, metal work and woodwork, of the highest quality and greatest beauty, they were preeminent, before foreign invasions deposed their old kings, who were the patrons of their arts and crafts.

The field of Hindu religion is so great that were we to assume all its material to be within the scope of yoga we would soon treble the size of this glossary, which would only trouble and confuse, and perhaps dishearten, those for whom it is intended. Yoga must be taken to mean a definite purposeful system of living (physically, emotionally, mentally, ethically and spiritually) and preparation for better living, with a view to the understanding, direct experience, and use of essential truths of life hardly noticed and certainly not consciously sought or used by the man or woman who merely drifts through life, as most people do, whether they be educated or uneducated, cultured or uncultured. Therefore, particulars concerning the passive and receptive religion of the masses have been excluded, and only terms giving information or instruction bearing upon self-culture and self-realization have been included.

When faced with the great number and variety of topics connected with yoga touched upon in this dictionary, the student may well exclaim: "What an immense mass and variety of things to know and to do!" Nevertheless, the pursuit of yoga is quite simple and straightforward. The student must not try to do many things; but must select and do one or two. The act of selecting is part of the work, and will be very useful if the student will allow himself to be intuitive, instead of being emotional about it. This glossary makes the subject look formidable because it contains the information and instruction given in many different schools; but really the aims are all the same three: to discover the Self, to lubricate the whole mind, and to make the body *sattwic*. Another point is that as a result of beginning and then carrying on the student will find perhaps to his own surprise and when he least expects it that he has attained something supremely valuable without knowing how.

Practical yoga could also be called the five-point way to health, for it shows how men should treat (1) their bodies, (2) emotions and (3) minds, and how they should cultivate their (4) ethical and (5) spiritual natures so as to have all these at their best and in perfect harmony with one another, so that these may serve as a chalice for the very Spirit or Self.

Ernest Wood

Pronunciation of Sanscrit words in this Book

Consonants generally as in English. *Th* never as in 'think' or 'bath,' but always as in 'penthouse.' *Ph* never as *f*, but as in 'haphazard.' Similarly with the *h* in *kh, gh, bh,* etc. *Jn* is usually sounded like *gny*.

Vowels are short if unmarked, but long when marked, thus:
a as in 'America,' *ā* as in 'father,'
i " " 'pin,' *ī* as *ee* in 'feet,'
u " " 'put,' *ū* as *oo* in 'cool,'
e " " 'prey,' *ai* as in 'aisle,' *o* as in 'hole,' *au* as ow in 'house.'
The note *q. v.* means "which see."

YOGA DICTIONARY

A

Abhinivesha.

Possessiveness, by some restricted to love of bodily life. Contains both desire and aversion in the form of attachment to things and life, and fear of loss and death.

Abhyāsa.

Persevering practice aiming at steadiness in yoga.

Absolute, The.

That which cannot be described in terms of matter nor in terms of mind, and yet must be the source and origin of both. This does not mean a void, for a void is something of the nature of material. It may be called pure consciousness, because consciousness is aware of both matter and mind, but since our present consciousness is aware of them as two and not as one, our consciousness does not know itself but only its reflection in this duality, though it may come to know itself, which is the purpose of yoga. It may also be called life, because life is what appears in consciousness in the coming together of matter and mind, so in the perfect meeting of the two in consciousness, that is, in the perfection of living, it may be experienced. This again is the aim of yoga—a perfection of living, which is to be exquisite, but not exclusive.

The absolute is the goal of yoga in practice because the yogī is taught not to predict his aim but to expect something of which he does not previously know. He turns his eyes towards that Being *(Purusha)* that was, as his *Rig Veda* puts it, "when there was neither entity nor non-entity," yet "whose members are the universe, and who, sacrificing himself, produced the *Veda* and everything besides." The yogī who falls short of this goal has, while still on his way, the reward of richer life—not necessarily richer material being nor necessarily richer mental being—which is relative freedom, and exquisite joy as compared with the imperfect pleasures of the body and the imperfect happiness of the mind, and this richer life contains the promise and increasing dawnlight of the goal. (See also under *Brahman* and *Sat-chit-ānanda).*

Abstinences. (yama), The Five Practices of.

These are abstinences from injury, untruth, theft, sensuality and greed. This puts the yogī at peace with the world, even if the world is not at peace with him. In the fourth abstinence there is generally special emphasis with regard to sexual conduct. It is to be understood that these are abstinences in thought and speech, as well as in deeds.

When successful, these five result in absence of hostility, effectiveness of speech and action, the arrival of what is needed, the development of vigor and the power to teach yoga, and the understanding of conditions and circumstances. The general belief is that the good man has nothing to be anxious about, except what arises from his own folly.

Actor, The.

The simile of the actor conveys the lesson that while the man is working hard at the

2

perfection of his present personality and its duties in the world he may forget that he is the actor and not that part which is being played on the stage. The *Bhagavad Gītā* strongly emphasizes the teaching that through doing his own natural duties in life he can best reach perfection, but in this he has to be the ruler, not carried away by the impulses of the lower self.

Adhi.

A prefix meaning above or over. It appears principally in such important words as *adhyātma, adhidaiva, adhibhūta* and *adhiyajna,* or, as regards the first three, in adjectival form as *adhyātmika, adhidaivika* and *adhibhautika.* For example, popularly, *adhyātmika* troubles and difficulties are those which arise from onself (see *ātmā), adhidaivika* those caused by planetary influences (see *deva),* and *adhibautika* those which are caused by outside agencies, such as tigers or snakes (see *bhūta).* But the student will see in the three terms a reference to the three great over-all or underlying Powers of the entire universe, which maintain respectively the inner self (*ātmika*), the mind-side or life-side of the whole creation *(daivika),* and the matter-side of creation *(bhautika).* He will also see that they correspond to the triple classification of man into spirit, soul (or mind in the full sense, including will, love and thought) and body.

The term *adhikārī* refers in yoga circles to one who is undertaking research and training with reference to these matters. It means one who is competent to direct his activities correctly, or, a qualified aspirant to yoga. In popular speech the term *adhikārī* indicates a foreman, a business manager, or a director of any affairs.

Adhyāropa.

Illusory attribution, such as

the mistaking of a piece of rope on the ground for a snake.

Adwaita.
(Literally, the non-dual).

That to which there is no second. A term used in Vedanta in reference to Brahman. The monistic Reality, which has the nature of Unity.

Ahankāra.
(Literally the "I-maker").

This is metaphysically the attribution of the reality that is Unity to something separate or a part. It is that fundamental error of the mind which causes it to regard anything as a unit, or an individual, or an entity. The term is commonly used for that habit of mind by which we ascribe to the bundle of objects and attributes comprising our body and mind the character of an entity, and then call it "myself," an expression which belongs properly only to the ātmā (*q.v.*).

Ahimsā. (Non-injury).

The first of the Abstinences (*q.v.*). The desire and endeavor to live and act at all times in such a way as to cause benefit and certainly not injury to others. It is not a strenuous campaign that is proposed, but more that our lives should be, in Buddha's phrase, "like soft airs passing by." The conception is, however, very comprehensive, including non-injury to people's thoughts and feelings as well as to their bodies and possessions, and non-injury by speech or even in thought, as well as by action.

Ajapā Mantra, The.

The involuntary or sub-conscious repetition of "hansa, hansa . . . " (*q.v.*) made by the breath, regarded as going out with the sound of ha, and coming in with the sound of sa. It is considered that this occurs usually 21,600 in the day and night, or 24 hours, which gives 15 per minute. In this connection it is interesting to note that the more excitable an animal is the quicker is its breathing, *e.g.* a hen about 30 times per minute, a duck 20, a monkey 30, a dog 28, a cat 24, a horse 16, a tortoise 3.

The act of breathing is often thought of as a reflection in the human body of that universal or cosmic creative movement by which the whole manifestation is periodically surged out and withdrawn (see under *Pralaya*). It is then considered that this *ajapā mantra* is an unconscious form of devotion or prayer in which *hansa (aham sah)* means "I am That" and *soham (sah aham)* means "That is I." (See also *Tat Twam Asi*).

Ājnā Chakra, The.

The wheel or lotus at the eyebrow level. This has only two petals, bearing the letters *ha* and *ksha*. It belongs to the mind in its character of "sixth sense," and is also referred to as in the region of the "moon," whence "nectar" flows down cation of the mind. This 'hap- the entire canal to enhance all the senses. It is also called *tāraka* (starry).

The yoga practice in this center is of two kinds, *mūrti* and *amūrti* (formed and formless). The earlier, the *mūrti* or *tāraka*, goes through all the senses, but the later, the *amūrti*, called *amanaska* (beyond thought) is above the senses, beyond the eyebrows and leads to internal vision and knowledge of the heavenly world where Indra presides. Hence the voice of the spiritual *guru (q.v.)* may be heard. In this *chakra* the bīja mantra *(q.v.)* is *Oṁ*.

Ākāsha. (Ether).

A kind of matter freer than even air, just as water is freer than earth, and air is freer than water. Inasmuch as objects partake of and associate with ether they can have separation and distance from one another.

Alinga.

That which has no attributes or characteristic marks *(linga)*.

5

Hence the Supreme Being, the same as the *Parabrahman* of the Vedantins and the *Paramashiva* of the Yogīs, or the Para *(Parama-Vishnu)* of the *Bhagavad Gītā.*

Alligator, The.

The lesson of the alligator is that one who lives merely to please his own body is like a person who sets out to cross a river on an alligator, mistaking it for a log of wood.

Anāhata Chakra, The.

The wheel or lotus at the level of the heart. It has 12 petals of a golden color (some say deep red), bearing the letters k, kh, g, gh, n (guttural), ch, chh, j, jh, n (palatal), t (cerebral) and th (cerebral). The animal here is an antelope; symbol of the sensitiveness, gentleness and fleetness of the movements of the heart or higher love, which is also wisdom. This is the center for the element air, of hexagonal shape and a dark blue color. The bīja-mantra is *yam.*

In this chakra the living man is said to move, like a spider on a web and very self-conscious, until at last he attains the very essence of *buddhi (q.v.).* The deities to be served in this and the two chakras next above will be of the Vishnu type, concerned with kindness, goodness and harmony, subject to three sub-aspects representing again Vishnu, Shiva and Brahmā.

Just below this center or within it, is another, smaller, having eight petals, often used for meditation on the *ishtadevatā* or the *guru (q.v.)* without reference to the other chakras or to kundalinī. The usual course here is to place one's consciousness in the heart (instead of, as usual, between or behind the eyebrows) and find or picture in that place an idyllic scene such as that contained in the following translation from the *Gheranda Sanhitā:*

"Let him find in his heart a broad
ocean of nectar,
Within it a beautiful island of
gems,
Where the sands are bright golden
and sprinkled with jewels.
Fair trees line its shores with a
myriad of blooms,
And within it rare bushes, trees,
creepers and rushes
On all sides shed fragrance most
sweet to the sense.
"Who would taste of the sweetness
of divine completeness
Should picture therein a most
wonderful tree,
On whose far-spreading branches
grow fruit of all fancies—
The four mighty teachings that
hold up the world.
There the fruit and the flowers
know no death and no sorrows,
While to them the bees hum and
soft cuckoos sing.
"Now, under the shadow of that
peaceful arbour
A temple of rubies most radiant
is seen,
And he who shall seek there will
find on a seat rare,
His dearly Beloved enshrined
therein.
Let him dwell with his mind, as his
teacher defines,
On that Divine Form, with its
modes and its signs."

Ānanda.

Bliss or joy. A characteristic of the pure consciousness which is the basic reality or substance of everything, called Brahman (*q.v.*). (see also under *Sat-Chit-Ananda*).

The term is also used to designate the bliss which is enjoyed in the *Ānandamayakosha* (*q.v.*) when the yogī's consciousness is raised into that.

Ānandamayakosha.
(See under Kosha).

Ananta.
(Literally, the endless).

A name given to the great coiled-up snake on which Vishnu is supposed to recline, according to the Pauranic stories. This is a symbol for an eternity of time—an aeon or duration or period in which some idea in the mind of Vishnu is intended to come to its perfection or ideal or archetype or fulfillment.

7

The yogīs are sometimes advised to call to mind this Endless when embarking upon a meditative undertaking, because they, of all people, must not be ruled by time, but must realize that they are doing something which makes time rather than takes time. All the undertakings of all the minds make all the time there is. In other words, the yogī has infinite or endless patience and perseverance, and keeps to his self-imposed task until it is done. Time helps him, because he can have as much of it as he wants.

The serpent-couch is also called *Ādi-shesha,* and is represented sometimes with a thousand heads and sometimes with seven heads.

Anātmā.

The not-self, which is the entire world of manifestation, both objective and subjective. Its use is as a friendly opponent to the higher self in the game of life, drawing out its

powers, until at last the final insight *(viveka, q.v.)* arises through which the consciousness is released from error or *avidyā.* (See also under Self).

Angas. (limbs of yoga) the Eight.

These are abstinences *(yama)*, observances *(niyama)*, seat or posture for meditation *(āsana)*, breath-control for meditation *(prānāyāma)*, withdrawal from the senses *(pratyāhāra)*, concentration *(dhāranā)*, meditation *(dhyāna)*, and contemplation *(samādhi)*.

Annamayakosha.
(See under Kosha).

Antahkarana.
The internal instrument.

The vedantic term for the whole mind, which lies between the Self *(ātmā)* and its external instrument, the body. The antahkarana consists of four functions:

Ahankāra: that which gives identity or "i-ness" to the ideas in the mind, including the idea of oneself.

Buddhi: that which gives a valuation to the ideas, and the facts which they represent.

Manas: that which compares and classifies the ideas and pictures of objects in the mind, and thinks about them.

Chitta: that part of the mind which is immersed in the world, and collects and stores the mental images; sometimes called the lower mind.

Apāna.

That *Vital Air* (*q.v.*) which is described as at the basic centre (see *Mūlādhāra Chakra*), near the anus, connected with the sacral plexus, and concerned with all the business of elimination of waste material from the body—in faeces, urine, perspiration, carbon dioxide etc. It appears to be of a red or orange color.

Aparigraha. (Non-greed).

The fifth of the Abstinences (*q.v.*). There is a proper measure of taking, holding and using all things—food, clothing and shelter for the body, company and friendship for the affections, instruments for edupy medium" should put one at peace with the world, and at ease in one's environment. "The middle way" is the best, as is shown by the fact that pain lies at both extremes— as when the bath water is too hot or too cold. This is not the same as Contentment— the second of the Observances (*q.v.*), though it does involve the idea of non-dependence on things and a willingness to let things come and go, and to "live on the wing."

Apavāda.

Withdrawal of *adhyāropa*. (*q.v.*)

Ardhamātra.
(Literally, half measure).

The sound which is at the end of the word *Om*. Generally the term refers to the half of a short syllable indicated by a dot on top of the word *Oṁ (q.v.)*.

This aftersound occurs also at the end of many mantric words. It is often printed as m with a dot over it. Some writers try to express it by ng, mentioning that there is no g in it, but there is the sound of the n as it would be if followed by a g. The m indicates that the lips are to be closed before the sound begins. In this book, whenever short mantras ending in this way are given, as in the descriptions of chakras, we have printed it simply as m, as in yam, lam etc.

Arhat.

In Buddhism, one who has attained a correct understanding of the nature of the beyond, and so is competent to complete the business of life by perfecting it, and releasing himself from five "fetters" which still bind him, namely the desire for life in form, the desire for formless life, spiritual pride, self-love and the last lingering remnant of ignorance or error.

For the attainment of the *arhat* condition the novice or aspirant has to throw off five simpler fetters, which are (1) the idea that the body itself is important and the feeling of being attached to it for its own sake, (2) doubt or uncertainty about the path to liberation, (3) dependence upon outward rules or forms or ceremonies, (4 and 5) likings and dislikings coming from the past, as habits impulsive in the present.

It will be seen that the ordinary man has to free himself from five objective bonds, and the arhat has to free himself from five subjective bonds. (See also under *Bodhi*).

Artist, The.

The simile of the artist conveys the lesson that while striving to paint a picture he is really trying to get a state of consciousness, and therefore he is really developing his own higher self or his own sensibilities and powers. Then it is seen that the picture is temporary and the man is permanent, and indeed that all work done in the world is really "for the sake of the self."

Āsanā. Sitting or Posture.

According to Patanjali, it should be steady and pleasurable. It is to be attained by removal of effort and the correct attitude of the mind, which has grasped what bodily poise means by a thought of the perfectly endless quietude of the basis of all things. In this condition of balance or poise, which involves no conflict or compensation of muscular energy, the body may remain very happily seated for a long time without fatigue and without being easily disturbed by outside changes.

Patanjali prescribes no particular posture, but later writers, especially of the hatha-yoga schools, list eighty-four of them, of which four and sometimes six are especially recommended for use in meditation. If the western student wishes to use a chair there is no objection, but for poised sitting the seat should be firm and of such height that the underside of the thighs may be horizontal, thus providing the feet to support the weight of the legs and the buttocks the body. The arms should hang vertically as far as the elbows, and then the hands rest anywhere on the thighs, according to length. The abdomen should be drawn in, while the shoulders are brought sufficiently back to allow free play of the lungs, and the neck and head should then be brought into line by imagining a pull or lift from above. In general, one should sit up, not sit down, but with no stiffness—rather with the maximum of relaxation, which can become almost complete when balance is achieved and the muscles of the neck and back (which are often unevenly developed by carelessness in ordinary life) acquire proper habits and their proper proportions of strength.

The postures chiefly recommended for meditation are given under *Siddhāsana, Padmāsana, Swastikāsana, Vīrasāna* and *Sudkhāsana*. Some other postures recommended as exercises for health and suppleness of body are given under *Bhujangāsana, Dhanurāsana, Halāsana, Kukkutāsana, Mayurāsana, Sarvāngāsana, Shavāsana, Shīrshāsana, Ugrāsana* and *Vrikshāsana*.

These latter postures are not meant to be held for a long time, as are the meditation postures, but are done as exercises, and held in some cases for only a few seconds. There are, of course, endless modifications of them possible, so those who practice them may find out for themselves variations which are beneficial.

Asat.

The unreal. (See under *sat*).

Āshrama.

A hermitage, or dwelling-place of persons (generally a teacher and his pupils) devoted to the religious life.

Also any one of the stages or phases of a lifetime—the first phase being connected with learning and study in preparation for the responsibilities of adult life; the second being that of the householder or family man; the third being that of retirement from active business, and of thought and study relating to the inner nature of man; and the fourth (when reached at all) one of renunciation (*sannyāsa, q.v.*) of all worldly desires and ambitions.

Life in the modern world also normally presents four stages of approximately 21 years each, in the first of which physical interests and developments predominate, in the second emotional, in the third mental, and in the fourth an understanding of the value of the synthesis of the three.

Asmitā.

Self-personality or egoism. The mistake of regarding the seeing of something as being the seer or looker, who is, however, pure consciousness, not consciousness which something has, even though it be a subjective something called oneself.

Asteya. (Non-stealing).

The third of the Abstinences (*q.v.*). As this virtue covers thought as well as act, it includes absence of covetousness and envy.

Ātmā or Ātman.

The true Self, in contrast with the false self of individuality and personality which each man commonly thinks himself to be. In Vedantic philosophy this is the one ever-present universal spirit, free from all conditions or charac-teristics of subject or object, of mind or matter, though it commonly appears to be a separate self, the *jivātmā* (*q.v.*) The equivalent reality in Sānkhya philosophy is *purusha* (*q.v.*), but in this case *purushas* are regarded not as one, but as innumerable. In these high regions of our thought, however, beyond the categories of mind and body, variety and unity are indistinguishable. There is also another term, the *pratyag-ātman,* which draws attention to the inwardness of *ātmā, pratyag* here meaning the inner.

Ātma-yoga.

That wherein the automat-ism of the lower mind (*chitta*) ceases, controlled by the practice of this yoga, and wherein, seeing the self by the self, one rejoices in the self—says the *Bhagavad Gita.* The same work further advises that, having made the higher mind (*manas*) *ātmā*-seated, let the man not think upon anything. If the *manas* wanders away he must lead it back into the power of *ātmā.* Then, united with *ātmā,* the yogī easily absorbs the unlimited happiness of contact with Brahman. He sees the *ātmā* standing in all beings, and all beings in the *ātmā*—everywhere the same seeing. Seeing the same everywhere—whether there is pleasure or pain—that yogī is considered the highest.

Attention without Tension.

A maxim in *rāja-yoga,* in which the development and use of the *inner man* is the aim. Especially is it important in the practices of concentration and meditation, for the success of these and for non-injury to body and brain.

Aum. (See under Om).

Āvarana. (See under Māyā).

Avasthās, the three.

These are three states of consciousness which all men experience:

(1) The Waking State (*jāgrat*), in which one is aware of the objects of the external world, and able to think and act in regard to them;

(2) The Dreaming State (*swapna*), in which there are only subjective or mental pictures of things, without rational control of them, and without any bodily pains or pleasures and mental appraisal of things;

(3) The Deep Sleep State (*sushupti*), in which there is nothing to be seen, either subjective or objective, but only a condition of blissful rest which may be remembered as such on awakening.

A fourth (*turīya*) state is sometimes mentioned, it being assumed that while in the third or sleeping state the individual (*jīva*), though retired into the causal body (*kārana sharīra*), is still separated by his own ignorance from the true self (*ātmā*), but in this fourth state (*turīya*) that has been overcome and he has pure knowledge (*shuddha vidyā*). Beyond this is the fifth (*turyātīta*) in which there is complete union and equality of the *ātmā* (self) with the *paramātmā* (supreme self of all).

Avatāra.

A rare person in human history, whose soul or mind is not in process of evolution and reincarnation, but is specially formed by a descent into humanity from the spiritual or divine regions beyond our life. The general idea is that *avatāras* appear at specific points in world history when the cyclic course of events requires a change, which the *avatāra* will be considerably instrumental in effecting.

Āvesha.
(Entering another's body).

One must first loosen the causes of bondage to one's own body (desire, etc.), then know how the mind uses the body (by thinking of speaking, walking, etc.). In *āvesha* there may be merely an influence, or there may be full possession. An example of the first case would be when a disciple is lecturing, the master may give him ideas; in the second case the disciple may step aside while the master uses his body, leaving his own body asleep or in trance or awake with only mechanical reactions. The second case is akin to mediumship, but the disciple can stand as it were aside, be aware of what is taking place, and exert a continuous voluntary participation in it without interfering. An extreme case occurs when a yogī is becoming very old and feels the need of a new body, and it happens that somewhere a child or young person dies (in the natural course of things or by accident). The yogī dies suddenly from his old body and enters the new one, and thus avoids going through some of the earlier years. The dead child then revives, and incidentally the parents find in it some remarkable changes of character and ability. In this case, the yogī will probably lose while in the new body, or rather brain, the memory of his previous body and its experiences, though he will have it when out of the body in sleep or trance. To understand all this, it must be taken into consideration that the progressed yogī leads, as it were, a double life, one in the body and the other out of it.

Avidyā.

Ignorance or error. Fundamentally the mistake of regarding the temporary as eternal, the impure as pure, the painful as pleasant, and the not-self *(anātmā)* as self *(ātmā)*.

Avyakta.
(The Unmanifested).

From a verbal root meaning to anoint, smear, mark, decorate. *Vyanj* is to manifest or reveal. *Vyakta* is thus what is manifest. In the manifestation of Nature things are spread out before us, and thus are seen. They could not be seen by us if they were set before us all together and all at once, not separated, for we are capable of dealing with only a small portion at a time. This is the secret of life, whereby by the very restriction of life we are learning to live, by the restriction of being we are gaining the power to be, and by the restriction of knowing we are gaining the power to know—because our consciousness, thought, love and will, grow by exercise in these limitations. The belief of the rāja-yogī and the jnāna-yogī is that we shall ultimately be able to live the true free life of unmanifested (that is, unlimited) existence, beyond the two great veils of subject and object.

B

Beyond, The. (Para).

An important term used to indicate, without describing, the state beyond the field of manifestation.

Bhagavad Gita, The.

A great scripture of India, in which a divinely illuminated spiritual teacher is presented as teaching a very eminent man of the military caste the art of spiritual living. The book consists of eighteen chapters, each one dealing with a particular aspect of human life, and showing how in that particular a man can be whole man, and play on all the five strings of the human harp (physical, emotional, mental, ethical and spiritual) at the same time, with all in harmony. Its main themes are brotherhood and the progress of man to and into divinity, which is also undiluted happiness.

Gītā means "song," or "what has been sung." *Bhagavat* is a term of the highest regard, as *bhaga* is the sun, with all its purity, power and splendor, while *vat* (or *vad* before soft consonants) is a possessive affix, the whole word meaning one who is sunlike or godlike. Throughout the *Bhagavad Gītā*, Shri Krishna, who in it gives his doctrine, is referred to as the *Bhagavān* (masculine nominative form of *bhagavat).* The entire compound *"Bhagavad Gītā"* has therefore been translated by such expressions as "the Lord's Song," and, as Sir Edwin Arnold put it in his very famous translation, "The Song Celestial."

Bhakti. (Devotion).

This is generally thought of as devotion to God, and especially to God as the source of all good things, or the supreme Bounty and Goodness. In the contemplation of this goodness, the emotion of worship arises; there is a sense of relationship or communion with that Goodness, which goes on beyond the awareness that we have of our fellow human-beings (see under *buddhi),* to an actual awareness of the divine. In brief, it is held that we have innately the capacity (1) to be aware of things through the senses and to know them better with the faculty of thought, (2) to be aware of our fellow-beings and to know them better with the faculty of love, and (3) to be aware of the divine and to know That better with the faculty of devotion or worship. In true devotion or worship there is, of course, no selfishness, no begging, but only appreciation and love of God, and equally of course there cannot be the thought of God as a great material thing or bodily being, nor as a great super-man or mind. But in thinking of this experience, one must not lose sight of the fact that this brings to man something *new* and *beyond* the other two forms of experience, so that saints and sages, having this experience, but unable to describe it because there is nothing previous with which to compare it, have nevertheless said: "Now we have real being, real consciousness, and real joy, beside which all that went before seems not deserving of the name of being, or consciousness or happiness." Is it surprising that men should be able to rise to this level, and that there have been many of the best men who have testified to it, and that these also have declared that it is the height of wisdom to look for the good —and the God—in all experience? True devotion or worship contains no selfishness or expectation of reward or gain, but just as in true human love the only consideration is the welfare and happiness of the person loved, so here the desire is God's happiness (if one may so put it), although in both cases love gives great happiness to the one who loves, even if it is sometimes accompanied by pain due to ignorance.

Bhāva.

Describes an outward or manifest state of being. Thus among human beings there are classified three *bhāvas:*

(1) The *pashu-bhāva* (bound), the lower group who do not lead a religious or ethical life but are living selfishly for the mere pleasures of the body, speaking ill of others, and thinking grossly; it is a good thing, however, that these people have very little effectiveness in action, word or thought.

(2) The *vīra-bhāva* (strong, energetic, virile), the middle group, who have ambition and purpose, and are excitably responsive to environment and quick to plan and act with reference to gains or improvements; these are capable of initiative, in selfish as well as ethical works (as the case may be), and in particular features or items of self-culture.

(3) The *divya-bhāva* (of a divine kind, that is, independent in character but harmonizing in actions), who are thoughtful in action, arranging their affairs for an orderly result, cleanly, peaceable, considerate, intelligently effective and interested in a spiritual goal or union with the divine at all times and stages of life.

It will be noticed that these three correspond closely to the division of human dispositions into *tāmasic, rājasic* and *sāttwic (q.v.).*

Bhujaṅgāsana.
(The Cobra Posture).

Lie face down; place palms on ground near shoulders; rear up the head and shoulders as much as possible, arching the back.

Bīja Mantra.

The sound connected with the *tattwa (q.v.)* or material principle of a *chakra.* When it is uttered, it is followed by an aftersound which is a nasal m and is written as a dot over the letter; thus in the *mulādhāra* the *bīja mantra* is la, which with the aftersound is lam, the n (or m with a dot over it) being sounded in all such cases like the n in "ink," with the lips closed.

(See also *Ardhamātra*).

This is called the *vaikharī* sound, but this is only the most material expression of it; behind that is a subtle *(sūkshma)* form of it, called *"madhyama;"* behind that another called *"pashyanti,"* and behind that again, at the points where movement begins from rest, the form of it called *"para."* So the *bīja mantra* represents an original power coming into manifestation. The sign of the aftersound is called the *chandra-bindu.*

Bindu.
(Literally, a drop or a dot).

When "Om" is sounded there is a nasal effect, because the lips are not opened to make a regular m. This sound is called *nāda,* and is indicated in writing by a small crescent on top of the letter o. There is a dot in the crescent, which indicates the final stage in that *nāda,* in which it becomes very subtle and gradually dies away. The length of prolongation is entirely at the option of the person using the *Om.*

Bodha.

Wisdom or understanding, such as can be imparted to another who is being taught.

Bodhi.

Perfect knowledge. In Buddhism, a correct understanding of the nature of the beyond. This correct perception it is which marks the *Bodhisattwa* or *Arhat,* who has still, however, to perfect it through a short series of births, or, some say, the equivalent of the same in the subtle body.

Bodiless states. (See under Videha and Prakritilaya).

Body, Perfections of the.

These are described in various yoga books. Pantanjali gives them as correct form, beauty, strength, and very firm wellknitness. An Upanishad gives them as lightness, good complexion, good functioning, slenderness and calmness. In all this there is no suggestion of injurious asceticism. Some persons practice self-injury and neglect, but these are quite misguided, when not somewhat insane, and all that can be said in their favour is that they are acquiring more will power, which, however, could as well be gained by the old advice that one should do every day some thing or things that one does not want to do, such as beneficial exercises.

Brahmā.

Not to be confused with Brahman or Brahma *(q.v.).* This, in the Pauranic stories, is that aspect of the Divine Unity, or the God, whose undertaking is creation, in the sense of the revival and maintenance of the material side of things; or he is the substance-power, which includes matter, force and natural law. The present writer defines this work, or substance, as that power which brings the past into the present, or the operation of inertia, which is both static and dynamic. This whole world-picture is subject to constant modification by all the incarnate minds (which belong to Vishnu, *q.v.),* and the new picture is then the object of Brahmā's solicitude and sustenance. The world thus presents a state of "objective ideation," the objectiveness being provided by the ever-present power and work of Brahmā.

Brahmā is pictorially represented as sitting on a fully-blossoming lotus flower, rising, on a long stalk, from the navel of the great deity who is his source. This principle or God, with all his work (the matter-side of things), is thus thought of as being empowered and instructed by the great deity who is the uncaused cause and basis of all. The word Brahmā comes from a root which means "to expand." From this the student will see the relation of this power to the matter-side of things, which is characterized by extensity and space.

The attitude of the yogī towards this aspect or power of deity is one of opposition, since he has to overcome any tendency to be ruled over by the past, and has to learn to govern his body, emotions and lower mind *(chitta, q.v.)*, all of

which have the habit-character of matter.

The whole idea conforms very closely to the conception of the Third Logos, which grew up among the gnostic societies of the near East, and the early Christian Gnostics.

Brahmacharya. (Chaste conduct).

The fourth of the Abstinences *(q.v.)*. The term means essentially avoidance of sexual action and excitement. In keeping, however, with the general idea that during studentship one should refrain not only from sexuality but from all forms of sensual indulgence for the enjoyment of the senses, and in harmony with the other four Abstinences, all of which are to be interpreted in a very broad sense, this term can be described as non-sensual conduct. There is a strong and wide-spread belief that the energy of the body which is used up by sexual thoughts and excitement will be available for higher purposes when there is absention in both thought and act.

Brahman or Brahma.

The one absolute being, also pure consciousness and undiluted joy or bliss, which is the basis and source of everything and is the one self of all, and union with which is the goal of Vedantic yoga. In this pure state Brahman is spoken of as without qualities (*nirguna*), but inasmuch as Brahman is the basis and substance of the entire universe with all its variety he is also with qualities *(saguna)*. When, then, there is thought of Brahman with the Universe, That is called *saguna*. Another term for this is the *Shabda* Brahman, *shabda* meaning sound or word, implying that the basic force in the universe is sound, issuing as a word or command—*Logos* in Greek.

In the coming of Saguna Brahman from Nirguna Brahman there is the expression of certain powers termed *shaktis* and in the schools of *Tantrik yoga* and in popular thought and tradition these powers are represented as Goddesses and consorts of the three great devas, Shiva, Vishnu and Brahmā (q.v.).

Brahma-sūtras, The.

Famous aphorisms ascribed to the great sage Bādarāyana or Veda Vyāsa, setting forth the principal teachings of the Upanishads with reference to Brahman. They are also called the *Vedānta-sūtras*. They have been extensively explained by many classical commentators. In these sūtras or aphorisms, what are called "the great sayings" play a prominent part— such as *"Sarvam khalwidam Brahma."* (Everything verily is God), from one of the Upanishads, and *"Ekam sat viprā bahudhā vadanti."* (There is only one Reality—or God— though the sages speak of that variously), from the Rig Veda.

Brahmavidyā.

Or *brahmajnāna*. Knowledge of Brahman.

Brāhmin or Brāhmana.

A man of the highest caste. But the *Vajrasūchi Upanishad* and other Vedantic works define him not socially, but as anyone who is directly aware that he is the ātmā, and is therefore without desire for worldly objects, and without egotism.

Breath, Regulation of. (Prānāyāma).

This is the control of the manner of movement of inbreathing and outbreathing. It is stoppage only insofar as it is the stoppage at a certain point of the inflow and of the outflow, not complete stoppage, for in such a case there would be no need to mention outflow or inflow, but merely stoppage of breathing. Outflow, inflow and standing still are the three items to be regulated by place, time and number. Number has reference to the proportions of the three items of breathing. One unit of time for inbreathing *(pūraka)*, four units for allowing the breath to remain inside *(kumbhaka)*, and two units for expiring *(rechaka)* is a much favoured ratio, but Patanjali, leaving the student to find his own standard of comfort and health in the matter, which differs with different persons, does not mention this ratio of 1:4:2 or any other ratio. In this matter of timing we have to consider the unit and the number of units. In older times—and even now—a favoured unit or measure *(mātrā)* was the time taken by a man in turning up his hand over his knee three times and then snapping the fingers, without haste. This seems to be about 3 seconds of modern clock and watch time. After a little practice the sense of length of one's chosen unit becomes habitual. The shorter unit of time often men-

24

tioned in Sanskrit philosophical literature, though not used in *prānāyāma* is called the second or moment *(kshana)*, and is often considered to be equal to one quarter of the time taken up in shutting an eye. With regard to both the unit and number of units of time to be used Patanjali makes no prescription. He remarks only that the breath should become long, *i.e.*, longer than usual, and— with regard to space or place— it should be fine, *i.e.*, not disturbing the air much or for any distance, the object in view being to have the body in a healthy and quiet condition, so that the covering of the inner light may be diminished, and there may be an undisturbed practice of mental concentration.

Breathing, Unusual Forms of.

The hatha-yoga books give many breathing exercises, just as they give many postures *(āsanas)*, and just as the latter falls into two groups—those

intended to train the body in good habits of sitting when meditating, and those intended as healthful exercises—so do the former. Good breathing is dealt with under *Prānāyāma;* here we give a very brief account of the eight exercises commonly taught:

There are many different practices of breathing advocated by various teachers of hatha-yoga, among which eight are usually mentioned, which are: (1) Practice *kumbhaka* (holding the breath) until the pressure of air is felt from head to foot, then breathe out through the right nostril; (2) breathe in deeply and noisily, hold as before, and exhale through the left nostril; (3) putting the tongue between the lips, breathe in with a hissing sound; exhale through both nostrils; (4) breathe out as fully as possible then in with a hissing sound and go on very rapidly like bellows until tired; then exhale by the right or (5) the left nostril; (6) breathe in with the sound of a male bee, and out with the sound of a female bee; (7) after breathing in, contract the throat, place the chin on the chest; breathe out very slowly; (8) simply hold the breath, without inbreathing or outbreathing, as long as you like.

Buddha.

That being who has perfected his *bodhi* or enlightenment, and is completely free from the bondage of the manifested state, both objective and subjective.

The Buddha from whose life and teachings the Buddhist religion arose, was a man of great insight and goodness who lived and taught the truths of his enlightenment about 2500 years ago in India. His family name was Gautama and his personal name was Siddhārtha. He used to refer to himself as the Tathāgata, which means one who has gone *(gata)* in that manner *(tathā)*, that is, who has fulfilled the noble eight-fold path *(q.v.)*, thrown off the ten fetters *(q.v.)* and arrived at *Nirvāna (q.v.)*, and is now composed, as it were, of wisdom *(bodhi)* itself.

Buddhi. (Wisdom).

Wisdom differs from mere knowledge because it is knowledge of the life-side of things. We live among two kinds of things—material objects and living beings, especially human beings. All things that are good for us are dear to us—we *like* them. But of all the things in our lives it is the co-human-beings who are the greatest and best "goods." Without them our lives would be poor indeed. Our feeling for these and our desire to cherish them becomes more than *liking*—it becomes *love*, in all its forms, beginning with friendliness and goodwill and going on to great affection. To be very conscious of the life in our co-beings is wisdom *(buddhi)*, and to estimate the value of all things only in relation to their welfare is also wisdom. (See also *karma-yoga* and under *antahkarana*.).

Buddhi-yoga.

A form of yoga much stressed in the *Bhagavad Gītā*. Indeed it appears, when one reads the book in Sanskrit, that almost always, when the Teacher mentions yoga without an adjective he means the *buddhi-yoga*. This is the yoga he first expounds to his pupil Arjuna, and which he later on states is that by which men reach the Brahman. When his pupil asks him what happens to a man who has faith in yoga but has failed in accomplishment because he has not sufficiently striven for it the reply is that this man who has fallen away from yoga will be reborn in a house of good people and will there obtain the *buddhic* attainments of his previous incarnation and again strive. To this the Teacher adds that the yogī is above the ascetics and the men of knowledge and action, and ends the topic by advising: "Therefore be a yogī." The reference to *buddhi-yoga* is very clear. Students of the *Bhagavad Gītā* may confirm this for themselves by reference to Chapter II, verses 39-41, 48-53, Chapter X, verse 10 and Chapter XVIII, verse 57.

C

Causal Body, The.
(Kārana Sharīra).

This is the first or inmost vehicle or body of the individual, and is also the first "sheath" *(ānandamayakosha, q.v.).* It is called causal because here is the individualizing power *(ahankāra, q.v.)* which starts off the whole process of limitation, manifestation or incarnation. It is related to the faculty of concentration *(q.v.),* and to the ignorance *(avidyā, q.v.)* which is the cause of all troubles *(kleshas, q.v.).*

Chakras, the Six.
(Literally, wheels).

Also called *padmas* (lotuses) because of their resemblance to that flower. The six chakras are described as threaded upon the subtle *sushumnā* (q.v.) channel within the spine at various levels in the body. The names and situations are:

1. Mulādhāra. At the base of the spine, near the anus.

2. Swadhisthāna. At the level of the genital organs.

3. Manipūraka. At the level of the navel.

4. Anāhata. At the level of the heart.

5. Vishuddhi. At the level of the throat.

6. Ājnā. At the level of the eyebrows.

Some modern scholars have strongly associated these chakras with important nerve plex-

uses in the body—notably
Major B. D. Basu of the Indian
Medical Service, who explained
these in his Prize Essay pub-
lished in the *Guy's Hospital
Gazette* in 1889. This eminent
doctor and scholar gave the list
as follows: (1) the sacral plexus, (2) the prostatic, (3) epigastric, (4) the cardiac, (5) the
pharyngeal, and (6) the caver-
nous.

The *padmas* are described as
having "petals," which indicate powers, which in turn are
indicated by letters of the Sanskrit alphabet. These, number-
ing fifty, are distributed in order, the number of letters, petals and therefore powers being
respectively: (1) four, (2) six,
(3) ten, (4) twelve, (5) sixteen,
(6) two. These petals could be
associated as Major Basu
pointed out, with the nerves
which are distributed from the
plexuses.

At the top of the *sushumna*
there is said to be the "thousand-petalled lotus," in addition to the six already mentioned. Major Basu associated
this with the medulla oblon-
gata, where the left and right
sympathetic cords have their
origin and are joined together.

Normally, as the yogic science depicts it, there is a certain amount of *kundalinī* force
always flowing up the channel,
but when more is awakened,
and the *chakras* are alerted
thereby, there can be an enhancement of the sensitiveness
of the senses and the powers
of action, amounting to clairvoyance, clairaudience, etc.,
associated especially with the
characteristic materials and
sensations, respectively as follows: (1) earth and smell, (2)
water and taste, (3) light and
sight, (4) air and touch, (5)
ether and sound, and (6) the
mind. A comparison can also
be made with the respective
principles of human activity as
follows: (1) body, (2) desires
and emotions, (3) lower or objective mind, (4) moral and
ethical nature, (5) the will, and
(6) the higher mind. Thus 1,

2 and 3 form a lower triad, connected with material affairs, and 4, 5 and 6 a higher triad, connected with the inner man. All these comparisons and connections have, however, to be interpreted in a very wide and free way, as the ramifications and inter-relations are as complicated as living itself, in which all our faculties take part in different proportions at different times. (See also under *Kundalinī,* and under the names of the *chakras).*

Character.

The good qualities of character which lead to liberation *(moksha, q.v.)* are thus given in the *Bhagavad Gītā:* Courage, purity of life, steadiness in *jnāna-yoga,* generosity, self-control, sacrifice, studiousness, austerity, uprightness, harmlessness, truth, absence of anger, renunciation, peacefulness, absence of slander, compassion for living beings, uncovetousness, gentleness, modesty, steadiness, heroism, forgive-ness, firmness, cleanliness, absence of malice, and not too much pride.

Charama shlokas.

The concluding verses of advice by Shri Krishna in the *Bhagavad Gītā:* "Be me-minded; be devoted to me; be worshipper of me; bow to me. You shall come to me . . . I promise, for beloved you are to me. Having cast aside all duties, to me, the one refuge, come . . . I will liberate you from all sins."

Along with this the pupil has to remember the teaching in verses given shortly before, that God is the same self equally dwelling in all, and the very spirit in the disciple himself is a share *(ansha)* of him. So there is no advice to look to another being for salvation.

Chinmātra.

The pure consciousness; "chit merely." The euphonic rules of the Sanskrit language require the t of chit to be changed to n when followed by m in such a compound word.

Chit.

Consciousness or knowing, which is ascribed to the one reality (see *sat-chit-ānanda*). Not to be confused with *chitta,* which is the lower mind, the fourth member of the *antahkarana (q.v.).*

Chitta. (The lower mind).

This is the mind which is to be controlled or rather, its contents are to be controlled. The *chitta* or lower mind is the mirror in which we receive and see all the pieces of sensation that come to us through the organs of knowledge *(jnanendriyas, q.v.).* In it they are kept for use, like the furniture in a house. All the information garnered during our life-time is here, available for our use (our thinking over) when required if the memory (smriti, *q.v.)* is good, which is the case when this mental furniture is well arranged in the mind.

There is, however, a dynamic or moving quality, as well as a static quality, about the ideas or pieces of information in the mind. They flow, by the association of ideas, in a routine manner, so that one idea calls up another, which is its successor, and that in turn gives place to a third, causing a flow or drift of ideas. This flow or drift is not to be confused with thinking (see *manas),* which governs and rearranges these contents of the lower mind.

Chitta-vritti-nirodha.

Control *(nirodha)* of the ideas *(vritti, q.v.)* in the mind *(chitta).* This leads through meditation *(dhyāna)* to contemplation *(samādhi),* which in turn leads through discrimination *(viveka)* to spiritual independence *(kaivalya).*

City of Nine Gates.

This refers to the body, which has two eyes, two ears, two nostrils, the mouth and two lower openings.

Cleanliness. (Shaucha).

Required of the aspirant to yoga as one of the five Observances *(q.v.)* prescribed for daily life in the world.

Clouds and Sun.

The simile of the clouds and the sun conveys the lesson that the shining of the true self is always present, but it is hidden by the clouds rising from the defects of the lower self or personality, so that not only its light cannot be seen but also its power cannot be enjoyed.

Concentration. (Dhāranā).

Is giving the full attention of the mind to any one thing or idea. Looked at externally, it is a narrowing of the field of attention, but internally it is the focusing of one's mental power. The practice of concentration is the doing at will what we commonly do spontaneously whenever we pay attention to any object or think of any idea, but the doing of it for a considerable time, permitting the mind to think only about the chosen subject, without wandering away from it along a line of associated ideas, as it commonly does.

The mind is to be thought of in two departments (1) the lower mind *(chitta)* which is like a workshop full of tools and materials (knowledge and memories), which, however, are in active associational flow or drift and (2) the higher or thinking mind *(manas)*, which is like a man who comes into the workshop and starts to make something new by combining the things which are there. In concentration the man stops the drift by paying attention to one thing.

For successful practice of concentration one must remember the following hints:

Let the object be naturally placed, as, a rose in a vase on a table, or growing on a bush —not floating in the air. Do not have a feeling of holding the idea of the object, but rather one of merely looking at it.

Attend to all the features of the object, with reference to sight, hearing, smell, etc. Let moving objects be moving, and still objects be very still.

Recall everything you can about the object, but do not think about these things except in their relation to the object— *e.g.*, if the object is a cat, by all means think of the cat drinking milk, but do not go away to the cow, certainly not beyond the cow.

Let the concentration be a calm, quiet poise—with no tension of either body or mind.

If intruding thoughts and feelings come up do not be unhappy about them, but merely remind yourself of what you are doing. The intruders will fade away if not attended to; they cannot be driven away or beaten down.

The object of the practice is to increase the power of attention, to establish the power to impose a mood of recall in the mind whenever desired (as opposed to the usual habit of drifting along and away) and to form a confident basis for thinking and meditation.

Consciousness (Chit).

This is something in us, or rather, which we really *are,* which is aware of both mind and body. We are conscious *of* the body, and indeed may feel and see it very strongly and clearly indeed. We are also conscious *of* the mind and its activities. Therefore our consciousness is not to be confused with either mind or body. Indeed, consciousness is simply *knowing,* which does not imply or require something or someone who knows. We are conscious *of* mind and *of* body, and both body and mind are unconscious.

Contemplation. (Samādhi).

Best known in common experience in rapture, when the *thought* of one's own identity ceases, (though not the consciousness) and there is unity of perceiver and perceived. It may be explained with reference to the fact that in all knowing of anything there is some unity of nature with that thing; *e.g.,* only because we are material in body we know material things; merely to have seen them and never to have felt or bumped into them would not have given us that knowledge. The same reasoning applies to emotions and ideas. It is only, *e.g.,* with our own ideas (part of our being) that we can understand other people's ideas. This reasoning is to be carried further, into ethics and spirituality, the latter being the root-being or share of original power which everything must have, the former being experienced in harmonious relations of these roots. As everything is unique it can deliver its message and impart its power to one who comes spiritually into tune with it, or contacts it (if the expression may be par-

doned) on the spiritual level.

The practice of contemplation supervenes upon meditation *(q.v.),* when the flow of thought comes to a natural end by the exhaustion of the stock of ideas, with (however) the continuance of the state of concentration, or by the inflow of intuitional contact or perception.

Thus it is that contemplation of anything can give new experience, and Patanjali mentions several examples, such as the elephant for strength—one would not know what strength is without experience, and one will know it more perfectly by entering into the very spirit of the elephant. Every small thing in Nature can give us its secret if we meet it in contemplation. There is rapture in the view of a great sunset or range of mountains for the common soul who needs a striking occasion, but there is rapture in the smallest thing for the man who has contemplation.

Contemplation cannot be

forced, nor attained by desire for an experience. It comes and grows by exercise.

It is the opposite of going to sleep. It can be called trance only in the sense that one is entranced with something, having been rapt away from attention to other things, but it is the greatest awareness or awakeness. It can be applied to the objective facts of nature, to the subjective facts of the mind and, at last, to the self.

Contemplation is of two kinds: cognitive *(samprajnāta)* and non-cognitive *(asamprajnāta)*. Cognitive contemplation has an object of thought, feeling or intention. It is accompanied by forms of (1) inspection or observation and enquiry regarding the object *(vitarka)*, (2) reasoning or investigation into its nature *(vichāra)*, (3) delight *(ānanda)* when some measure of success in finding the reasons for things, which is the harmony of things, is attained by means of the foregoing and (4) sense of enhancement of oneself, or sense of power *(asmitā)*. All attention to things has as its central aim the enhancement of one's own consciousness, and this is normally accomplished by the error of self-personality, the second of the sources of trouble or *kleshas (q.v.)*.

When the purpose of the contemplation is to gain a fuller, or more accurate or more unified knowledge of anything which has become focused upon, or to obtain knowledge of something about it which you have not yet known, there will always be in the background some desire for enhanced consciousness, which is called the sense of power. You are not carried away by some feature of the object which is attractive to you and gives you pleasure and awakes possessiveness. You are using the object to attain an inner state of mind, and you are so much master of the situation that you can make a complete job of your practice of contemplation, which is preceded by concentration and meditation. The very word *samādhi* (contemplation) implies this completeness, as it means, fundamentally, agreement—a co-ordination of the entire contents of your mind with reference to the object, leaving nothing out, and leaving no confusion or conflict in the mind. After the concentration and the meditation, when there are no more thoughts to put into their proper places in the unified picture, you continue your attention at the top end of your line of thought, as it were, which however is not a line but a ball, in a state of expectancy, awakeness, or alertness —the opposite of going to sleep. It is in this state that something new will arise, which will be an enhancement of the consciousness which will be the seed (see *bīja*) of a new interest, which will have in turn its action, object-enquiry and perhaps a new practice of concentration, meditation and

contemplation in the future. Such is the contemplation— with cognition, the object of which may be something seen or something merely read or heard about, which latter, to the Hindu mind means something scriptural, a description, perhaps, of something in an anticipated heaven.

The non-cognitive contemplation *(asamprajnāta samādhi),* however, depends upon a superior kind of uncoloredness *(paravairāgya).* In this case one is not seeking among the things which offer (1) stability, continuance, comfort, or (2) activity, change, adventure, or (3) harmony, peace, poise as the fruit of contemplative mastery. The whole mind has become so mature that it begins to be the receptacle of intuitions about the real man *(purusha q.v.).* This is not an object of thought, an idea, but an experience, so there is not merely a control *(nirodha, q.v.)* of the ideas in the lower mind, which is outward turned, but a cessation of the desire for enhancement because even that is something subjectively objective. It is, in western terms, the birth of the spirit, beyond the enjoyment of the soul. There is not any springboard for this; it is the taking hold of the downreaching hands of the real man, who is known with a knowledge beyond the kind of knowing which contains subject and object, which is of the mind, or soul. All that remains in the mind after such a contemplation is its own tendency or mood or habit-mold *(sanskāra)*, which makes the process easier and more successful in future practices.

Contentment. (Santosha).

Required of the aspirant to yoga as one of the five observances *(q.v.)* prescribed for daily life in the world.

D

Dama.

Pacification of the body, or rather of the ten organs *(indriyas q.v.)* of sense and action, so that they remain quiet when not called upon to function. One of the six attainments. (See under *shatsampatti).*

Dance of Shiva, The.

Shiva has many dances, but the one most commonly figured depicts him as treading on a dwarf. The dance is in general to remind us that the deity plays, does not work. The dwarf in this case is called "man of forgetfulness" *(apasmāra purusha),* which is of course that lower self of ours, and even to some extent the higher self, in which we become so involved that we forget our high spiritual calling and destiny, of which, however, Shiva reminds us through his quality of will in us, which is not merely a will to live, and a will to adventure and growth, but also a will to spiritual fulfillment.

Darshana.

To have *darshana* is to have a look at. This is a great blessing—to see a flower, a tree, a person. For that flower, tree, person, is living *for us,* and we drink in its attainments as well as our own. In yoga, *darshana* of the guru is considered in itself precious. Even though the aspirant can only see what he can, nevertheless his mood of respect and indeed reverence for all things is the exercise of his "can-ing," and provides for its growth, and as he progresses he may be able to see more of the "master-ness" in the master, and be less taken up with the man-ness of him.

But in this there must be no ulterior motive; the growth is only through the happiness which is in the seeing. The *rishis* (seers) had, and have, much of this.

The term *darshana* in course of time came to mean an outlook, hence a system of philosophy. The great *darshanas* of old India are given as six: the *Vaisheshika* (analysis of the universe), *Nyāya* (laws and facts of logic), *Sānkhya* (classification of the universe), *Yoga* (practice of union), *Mīmānsa* (laws of formal religion), and *Vedanta* (knowledge of God).

Death.

Mystically, it is this our embodied condition of life that is death, since it to such a large extent obscures and buries the true man. He is under great limitations, but on the other hand he learns good lessons one after another by this means. Even the dying of the body is beneficial, as it enables the soul to go on to a new and different lesson in the next incarnation. Thus the evolving being gradually fills up the deficiencies in his powers. Yoga is the learning of these lessons and the filling up of these deficiencies voluntarily, instead of being content with the slow process of Nature's simple schooling.

Deer, Elephant, Moth, Fish and Bee, The.

The lesson of these five animals is one of warning to beware of the attractions of the five senses, for the hunters lure the deer with soft music, the elephant is caught while rubbing itself with great pleasure against a tree, while the moth, the fish and the bee are lured by sight, taste and smell.

Deha.

Body. Man has three of these: the dense, subtle and causal. (See under Upadhi).

Dehī means "one who has a body," just as "yogī" means one who has yoga to some extent or in some degree. It does not mean (as sometimes translated) "dweller in the body," as it carries a sense of much more power than that, unless we think of the dweller in the house of the body as one who knows and can operate all the arts of building, for this dweller has a body which is the result of his own building, and he can make changes in it. The body is man's instrument for living in the outer or objective world, whereas a house is mostly a shelter into which to retire for privacy and rest, so the body is more like one of those repair-men's automobiles all fitted up with every tool that is needed than it is like a house; and since man's business in the world is to repair, recondition and improve his *jāti (q.v.)* which is the result of his past *karma (q.v.)*, the simile is very apt.

Deity,
Pictures and Images of.

These are very commonly used in temples, in home and in private meditation and shrine rooms. This is not idolatry when it is remembered, that they are not usually thought to be in themselves sources of benefit or power, but are reminders of divine things. A certain amount of leaning, or dependence, on divine assistance often comes into this devotion, but this is not illogical, for do we not lean even upon a flower and thank it for its calmness and beauty, which can infuse us with something of the same? The use of pictures and deities can strengthen the mind, and, if there are many symbols can widen the understanding.

Desire-Nature, The.

That part of the lower mind (q.v.) which is concerned with our feelings about objects, resulting from our opinions about them and our previous pleasures and pains in connection with them. This desire-nature *(kāma, q.v.)* gives excitement and strength to the relations between the mind and the objects of the world, resulting in knowledge inside and action outside, leading to more and more of this relationship until it becomes too much and the intelligent mind has to step in and curb or organize it.

Desires.

These are considered to be inimical to the achievement of yoga, when they are *vāsanās* (q.v.) or habits of desire arising from the past. "What grief springs of itself and springs not of desire?" — was Buddha's rhetorical question, showing that this is a matter seriously to be considered by the man who proposes to guide his life by reason towards happiness, and then he will see the folly of allowing his automatic responses to the challenge of the world to be governed by these impulses.

Devadatta.

One of the minor vital airs (q.v.).

Devas.

Divine beings, or beings above and beyond the human. Although *the* Divine Being, or Brahman, must be without any of the categories or characters of the manifested world, whether of the mind-side or of the matter-side of Nature, yogīs sometimes allow themselves to think of the divine causativeness in terms of such beings, as in the cases of the devas named Shiva, Vishnu and Brahmā *(q.v.)*. This is regarded as an aid to concentration and meditation. It would be an error, however, if they thought that such a being were real and

41

active as an entity in the world. Nature-spirits, and the psychic entities whose forms are maintained by human thought and devotional shrines are, of course, not devas, being far from divine, and worship of them is a great obstacle to the fulfillment of yoga.

Dhananjaya.

One of the minor vital airs *(q.v.)*.

Dhanurāsana.
(The Bow Posture).

Lying face downward, raise the legs backward, catch hold of the ankles with the hands, raise the head and chest. The body remains balanced on the abdomen.

Dharma.

From a root which means to maintain, support or sustain. When taken as rectitude, it means a way of life such that one does not slip back from the high standard of character and conduct which one may have reached previously. One must consolidate one's mental, moral and ethical gains. Thus dharma is duty to oneself, and it is also being true to oneself. Though taken by great thinkers to be an inward and spiritual law of duty, it is also taken by many to mean the upholding of outside social rules, such as the system of caste, which is now rapidly fading away in India.

Dharma is also taken as law or rule in connection with the numerous ceremonies in orthodox Hindu life. There are detailed directions regarding how to pray, to perform *pūja* (devotional submission) and *yajnas* (sacrificial ceremonies) to obtain specific results. These are held to constitute a whole science for dealing with the unseen world (*adrishta*) and unpredictable fate. The yogī, however, generally renounces these and proceeds to the full use of his own powers of mind, through concentration, meditation and contemplation. The Vedantic yogī goes to that limit in this respect; renouncing all material and egoic goals, he seeks only Brahman and turns his back even on heaven.

In Buddhism *dharma* appears as *dhamma*— the law or way of life prescribed by Buddha as leading to nirvāna (*q.v.*). Buddha's *dhamma* is the same as his "noble eight-fold path" (see under Path).

Dhautis. (Cleansings).

These are miscellaneous practices of the Hatha-yogīs similar to the *Mudrās (q.v.)* but in this case the object in view is the purification of the physical body, rather than the pursuit of psychic faculties and powers. These also are in many cases dangerous. They are not required in Rāja-yoga. They include such practices as: swallowing air into the stomach, retaining it awhile and expelling it from below and doing the same with water;[1] pressing the navel and intestines in toward the spine many times;[2] cleaning the teeth with a frayed twig or cane, with or without powder or earth, also cleaning the tongue and throat;[3] rubbing and pressing the forehead near the nose, and the depression at the bridge of the nose;[4] gargling;[5] swallowing a strip of thin cloth and pulling it out again;[6] cleaning the rectum with water;[7] sitting in deep water and sucking it through the rectum to wash out the bowels;[8] passing a thin thread in at the nostrils and bringing it out at the mouth;[9] looking without winking until tears flow;[10] drinking in water at the nostrils and sending it slowly out at the mouth and the reverse.[11]

[1] (*vātasāra and vārisāra*)
[2] (*agnisāra*)
[3] (*dantadhauti and jihwa-shodhana*)
[4] (*kapāarandhra prayoga*)
[5] (*vāma dhauti*)
[6] (*vāso dhauti*)
[7] (*mūlashodhanam*)
[8] (*jala vasti*)
[9] (*neti*)
[10] (*trātaka*)
[11] (*vyut and shīt kramas*)

Diet.

Though Patanjali makes no mention of diet, but leaves it to the good sense of the aspirant to yoga, there is much other Sanskrit literature which does give good advice. Generally a light diet of juicy, oily and bland food, is recommended, the stomach to be half filled with solid food, a quarter with liquid and a quarter with air. The book *Hatha-yoga-Pradīpika* recommends especially milk and butter, wheat, rice, barley, honey, dry ginger, cucumber and various vegetables. Garlic and onions are generally avoided, also anything bitter, acid, pungent, salty, or hot, intoxicants, fish, meat and eggs. There are, however, no hard and fast rules in these matters. Health without coarseness is the chief consideration, so the food should be nourishing, easy to digest, and free from bad thought-associations and bad "magnetism."

Direct cognition. (Aparoshānubhūti).

Realization. One cannot have knowledge of the Self, or of God, by mere inference, nor by the testimony of others. By inference there may be "knowledge about," but not the knowing required in yoga attainment, which must be direct cognition, analogous to the direct vision of material objects by the eye.

Disembodied state, the (Videha and Mahāvideha).

Deha is body; videha, bodiless; mahā, great. Generally when thinking of oneself even as mind, there is a thought of oneself as embodied or objective. To be without that thought is to be in one's state of excorporeal reality. This refers to the mind functioning away from the body (astral travelling etc.) and also to the more philosophical insight in which the mind (*manas*) functions in reference to something without thinking of itself as in any way related to it. In the latter case there is the removal of what acts as a veil or covering of the fullest intuition or direct vision with regard to the object, and of the real lucid knowledge of oneself.

Divinity, The Meaning of.

This word appears to come from far back, where in the Sanskrit language the verbal root *div,* to shine, is found. This is now applied to that which shines—not only with light but in any and every way —with its own power, not derived from any other source. This is held to exist as the basis of existence, as God, and also as the divinity of each man, as he has a share of that and is rooted in that. It is the truly spiritual, beyond mind as well as body. Often it is associated with the sun as a symbol, since the sun shines with its own light, while the moon, in contrast, shining only with reflected or borrowed light, stands for the limited, the manifest.

Drashtā or drashtri.

The Looker or Looker-on. The real man, who must come to reside in his own nature (*swarūpa*), instead of continuing to be misled into regarding himself as something else. This is nothing but consciousness, pure consciousness, and is the true being that we are *(purusha q.v.).*

Dreaming State, The.
(See under Avasthas).

Dreams.

A big subject, but one which has little place in the work of the yogī, because dreams are constituted mainly of the automatism of the lower mind and the emotional body (or set of habits) when the reasoning faculty of the positive or higher mind is in abeyance. In general they have healing value (to the mind), which resides in their free flow, however fantastic, by which incoherence or unco-ordinated emotions find their relational balance. They are like the disturbed forces in nature, as in a storm, which are violently seeking a balance (or peace) though they are not in themselves violent.

Into dreams may also come thoughts from others, and thoughts which have been left attached, as it were, to objects in the vicinity, such as in the room where one may be sleeping. There may also come in some experience received while "travelling in the astral" during sleep, which is done quite rationally by many people who have no memory of it in their waking state. In such a case, of which many celebrated examples are on record, the "dream" may contain some results of meeting and conversing with others as well as remembrances of things seen. The solution of problems during sleep is not by a passive sub-conscious mind, but as a result of something done in this condition. This travelling or working "in the astral" should not occupy all one's sleeping time, however, as the mental and emotional conditions need their relaxation in which to dream themselves into co-ordination. Beyond this, too, the positive triad or at least the higher *manas* (mind) needs its reflective (as contrasted with working) time for communion at its own level.

Drik.

That which sees the manifestation, including both the objective and subjective sides of it; therefore the Brahman *(q.v.)* or *ātmā (q.v.)*.

Drishya, The.
(Literally, what is seen).

The whole manifestation, including both the objective and subjective sides of it. Contrasted with *drik (q.v.)*, the seer.

Duality. (See Dwaita).

Duty. (Dharma).

What a man ought to do; the proper way for a man to live generally, and to act on particular occasions. The law of *dharma* stands over against the law of *karma* (*q.v.*), since the latter presents a man at every moment with a material situation, and then the question arises—what is he going to do about it? His first duty is to himself; he owes it to himself to use his own powers, for only by such use does he grow as a man. His second duty is to love his neighbor, in his heart and in action, in the social function or profession by which he contributes his share to the common welfare, which is considered to be the height of social service. His third duty is to God, since life and death exist only to fulfil union with the divine in full consciousness.

Dwaita.

Duality; the first effect of error (*avidyā*), or the power of illusion (*māyā*).

Dwesha. (Aversion).

This feeling of emotion arises from the memory of pain connected with any idea or object.

E

Egoism or self-personality. (Asmitā).

The second of the five *kleshas*, or sources of trouble.

Elements. (Mahābhūtas).

The five great elements of matter, or states of matter are called the *mahābhutas*. These are ether, air, fire, water and earth. But the elements known to us in the gross and visible world are not these five in their pure condition but a combination of them, in the following manner, which is called *panchīkarana:*

Gross earth has 50% pure earth and 12½% each of the other four.

Gross water has 50% pure water and 12½% each of the other four.

Gross fire has 50% pure fire and 12½% each of the other four.

Gross air has 50% pure air and 12½% each of the other four.

Gross ether has 50% pure ether and 12½% each of the other four.

Enthusiasm, The Danger of.

In yoga there is no excitement, and certainly no whipping-up of enthusiasm. There are two dangers in such "recharging of the batteries": (1) material aims concerned with bodily enjoyments or personal ambitions, and (2) drawing on your reserves. Very often people think they are sucking in power from the infinite when they are really drawing on their reserves.

The former simply delays one's inner progress (though indirectly they lead one into experiences—see under *karma* —which require the attention of the inner man). The latter often leads to some kind of bodily breakdown. Yes, one may feel just grand and "on top of the world"—but at what expense and with what dire results. In these matters the old proverb, to make haste slowly, is invaluable.

Etheric Double, The.

The material portion of the *prānamayakosha*. (See under *Koshas* and *Upadhis*).

Evolution.

A modern term which indicates an advance in a living organism in two ways—an increasing variety of limbs and organs, and an increasing co-ordination or harmony of their relationship. There is, of course, a concealed but necessary principle of unity at work also. This idea of evolution applies to the mind and its increase of knowledge, as well as to the body.

In yoga this evolution applies to the bodies (*koshas, q.v.*) of the yogī, and also to the fact that these are being changed from sluggishness (*tamas*) to restlessness (*rajas*) and from that to harmony (*sattwa*). But as regards the yogī's own inner progress the term purification is preferred to evolution, because that depends not on any action of the mind, but on the purification of it, so that the yogī becomes more and more aware of the grand possibilities of his own consciousness the more he becomes master of the field of work and the less he allows it to stain him with its lures or imperfections from the past. He is going on into the fulfilment of the future in a glorious present not yet attained, but destined.

Eyes, Relaxation of the.

In meditation the eyes must

not be strained. On account of habit there is a tendency to focus the eyes on an imaginary object, so it is best to unfocus them at the outset, which can generally be done simply by looking into the distance. A simple exercise is to put the two index-fingers together horizontally, tip to tip, at the level of the eyes and about book-distance away from them, then alternately look at their meeting place and away through them into the distance. In the latter case a third finger will be seen floating between them. The eyes may be closed while the third finger is in view. Once the feeling of relaxation is acquired the rest is easy.

Apart from meditation, it is desirable not to have the eyes tense when reading, etc.

It is also desirable to do some exercise which will give a little movement to the various muscles of the eyes. The following can be recommended: Without moving the head, let the eyes wander slowly, without jumping, along the outlines of the wall or scene in front. Move them up and down or to and fro on a line several times before changing the line. Take several lines in different directions, horizontally, vertically and diagonally, and, finally, round and round. Relax the eyes now and then.

F

Face, Relaxation of the.

After practicing the exercises for the neck *(q.v.)* one may do the following: Lean forward, letting the head loll downwards. Then relax the whole face, jaw, lips, cheeks, nose, temples etc., at the same time giving sharp little shakes of the head from side to side, but not severely, while you feel the whole face going out of shape, as it were, and hanging, and waggling loosely—even to the ears, nose, temples, and even in some cases the very scalp. After a few such shakes, sit up straight, stretch the neck upwards, and settle the head *(q.v.)*, after a few slight stretches in various upward directions, into a balanced position on the neck.

Nearly all persons will at once feel the benefit of this, and then normally, when they are looking at something, or reading, or walking along, they may remember now and then to relax the face—not, of course, into the complete relaxation taught here, especially if other persons are present, but into its own balanced musculature, without tension, which can become habitual.

Faith. (Shraddhā).

A virtue leading to the search for and reception of

something new to be derived from yoga practice. Taken along with vigorousness (*vīrya*), memory (*smriti*), the practice of contemplation *(samādhi)* and understanding (*prajnā*), all of which it energizes or inspires, it is declared to be one of the best means to pass on to the higher contemplation. Faith, however, is not mere belief, for it grows by repeated and increasing trials and fulfillments. It has the nature of confidence in himself and in the methods of yoga. This saves the yogī from attachment to objective or subjective goals, and the fear which accompanies the following of such goals.

"Fear not."

The first words of the *guru* or teacher to the would-be pupil (*shishya*) who has come to him for refuge from the troubles of material existence.

Fetters, The Ten.

In Buddhism, the ten defects to be overcome. (See under *Arhat*).

Field, The. (Kshetra).

A term used to indicate the whole field of manifestation and all the objects in it. Connected with this is the term "knower of the field" (*kshetrajnā*), which refers to the self or *ātmā*.

Fire-walking.

This occurs at various places in India at certain seasons. It is an example of the power of mind over matter, and so is related to yoga, though yoga goes further and deals with the power of spirit over mind. A typical case of fire-walking was that shown in England some years ago by Kuda Bux. Two trenches were formed, 12 ft. long, 6 ft. wide and 8 inches deep. In these seven tons of oak logs, one ton of firewood and 10 gallons of oil were set alight and allowed to burn for several hours so as to become glowing embers, which showed a temperature of 800° F. Bux had his bare feet examined and then walked twice through the trenches, without harm. Paper which happened to blow across the trenches immediately burst into flames. Bux could only explain it as a matter of faith. All our abilities are, of course, ultimately that.

Forces.

This term is used in four distinct ways in connection with yoga and occultism.

(1) The forces of Nature. These are seen in the adjustment of material equilibriums, and are what are usually studied in the science of physics— heat, light, sound, electricity, magnetism, etc.

(2) The forces in the etheric double, particularly the vital airs (*q.v.*) and *kundalinī* (*q.v.*).

These also are within the field of material Nature.

(3) The forces exerted by thought-forms and emotion-forms, which, though generated by the mind, become, on issuing from their creators, independent entities charged with emotional and mental forces until they die away. These also are in the field of material Nature, although in the subtle regions at the level of the lower mind.

(4) Living entities such as human beings are also called Forces, because they can by their own powers of thought, love and the will, introduce changes in the three departments of Nature already mentioned. It is here that *kriyā-shakti* and *ichchāshakti* (*q.v.*) come in. (See also under *Shakti*).

G

Gāyatrī Mantra, The.

One of the most important of all *mantras,* formerly used only by Brahmins, which runs: *"Om, bhūr, bhuvah, swah; tat savitur varenyam bhargo devasya dhimahi; dhiyo yo nah prachodayāt. Om."*

The meaning of the main part of the *mantra* is: "We meditate on the ineffable effulgence of that resplendent Sun; may That direct our understanding." The use of "we" and "our" is interesting as showing a desire for the benefit of others, presumably all who share in this aspiration. Sun, is, of course, a symbol for divine mind.

The mention of the three regions (*bhū* etc.) at the beginning is usual, though some carry it further and mention seven. Ordinarily, these refer to our physical, emotional and lower mental states, wherein the effect is desired. Higher states are those *from* which one is to receive, not *into* which one's thought is to be projected.

God.

Although the idea of God has no part in the *Sānkhya* philosophy on which the Rāja-yoga is based, Pantanjali introduces the conception and defines God as a specific *puru-*

54

sha (q.v.) who is unaffected by any container of the sources of trouble or *kleshas (q.v.)*, by actions or by the results of fruition of actions—in short, an independent being, the uncaused cause of whatever he does or knows, the teacher of the old teachers, unlimited by time.

It will be noticed that this is a *purusha* having independence or *kaivalya (q.v.)*, so it is implied that the yogī attaining independence becomes such a god. The advaita Vedantins and the *Bhagavad Gītā* plainly say that the yogī achieving liberation *(q.v.)* finds himself one with Brahman *(q.v.)* which is another term for *īshwara* or God. The *Bhagavad Gītā* further avers that at all times each man's *īshwara* is a share of Brahman which is the very root and support of all his being. Contemplation of such a being is the nearest thing to a goal that the yogī can formulate. Patanjali recommends the aspirant to repeat the sacred word *"Om," (q.v.)* which indicates but does not name *īshwara*, with thought upon its meaning.

God, Approach to.

Four terms are commonly used for increasing degrees of this:

Nearness *(samīpya)*,
similarity *(sārūpya)*,
being with *(sālokya)*, and
conjunction *(sāyujya)*.

The last is equivalent to liberation *(q.v.)*.

Good, The Highest. (Paramārtha).

There are many goods in life—goods for the body, the emotions, the mind and for the exercise of our higher faculties; but the supreme good (realization of the presence of the spirit, and the real self which that is) is to be sought. This the yogī has in view, and to this *jnāna-yoga* he should give some of his time and attention, as well as to the *rāja-yoga* needed for the higher self, and also to whatever practices may be necessary to correct the condition of the lower self in the three departments of body, emotions and lower mind.

Goodness, Truth and Beauty.

The three Greek ideals, which were formulated as the external basis of civilization. Truth is honesty in thinking, as seen in science; goodness is love, in neighbourliness, brotherhood, philanthropy and religion; beauty arises from skill in action, assisted by the perseverance of the will. Truth promotes our intimate contact with materials, love with persons, the will with the body and its works. In human life these three kinds of work indicate the presence of the inner man.

Granthis, The.
(Literally knots).

There are three of these; in the basal *(mulādhāra)*, heart *(anāhata)* and eye-brow *(ājnā)* *chakras*. It is explained that *kundalinī* has to break through these knots in the course of her journey up the spine. The first is sometimes called the knot of Brahmā, the second that of Vishnu, the third that of Shiva. There are three states through which the human consciousness has to go before reaching perfect union with its own true self, or the abolition of bondage. The first compares with the first three *chakras* (which are concerned with physical, emotional and lower mental interests), the second with the next group of three (the higher mental, *buddhi* and *ahamkāra*, of which the *buddhi* is the focus, being concerned with the perception of operational consciousness as distinguished from the sense of material being which the consciousness enjoys in the first three), and the third with the real self beyond even the operational consciousness. As long as the consciousness thinks of itself as operational (of thought, love and the will) it is in bondage to that, practices that and enjoys that, and is what is sometimes called the higher self. But it must break through that by the highest discrimination *(viveka)*, which destroys the last remnant of that ignorance *(avidyā)* by which in the consciousness the inner man or higher self is mistaken for the real self. Every yogī becomes a Vedantist at this point, where his thoughts and understanding make the final perception by which they yield up their own sovereignty, and thereby release the consciousness, which then knows itself as itself.

Gunas.

Qualities of Nature. These are three, stability *(tamas)*, restlessness *(rajas)*, and orderliness *(sattwa)*, which see. The development of beings in Nature proceeds through three stages which correspond to these. This applies to men also. At first there is sluggishness; then, through sluggishness, neglect, and, from neglect pain (as, *e.g.* hunger or cold). Next from pain effort results, from effort experience of pleasure (as, *e.g.* the taste of food). From this arises the seeking of pleasure, energetic action, and, as this becomes a habit, restlessness. Next, from excessive pleasure-seeking and pleasure-getting pain again arises. This gives occasion for thought, which observes the facts and laws of Nature, and establishes moderation, proportion, harmony and orderliness.

Guru.

In the old books there is the frequent advice to the aspirant to yoga that he (or she) should obtain information and instruction from a *guru* or teacher. The word *guru* means literally "a weighty person," one whose words are worthy of the most respectful consideration; not a dictator but a consultant. In modern days books have largely taken the place of the gurus, and many people are getting much benefit by the practice of selected portions of the yoga teachings, which they follow with discrimination and in moderation.

H

Habit.

Most living is by habit,
which our consciousness accompanies, and enjoys because
of absence of effort. The inner
man, however, works a little,
to alter the habit-pattern, by
means of thought, love and the
will. The cultivation of these
three directly is the first part
of yoga, which continues until
they become somewhat mature
(they are still almost tentative
in many people), when the
intuition of the very self arises
and a new element is added in
consciousness, namely, knowledge of the spirit or self, in
addition to the former knowledge of body and mind or soul.

Habit-mold, or Mood. (Sanskāra).

A *sanskāra* is a habit-mold,
or mood governing the flow of
thought at any given time.
When the will so determines,
there is a transformation of the
lower mind *(chitta)* itself into
a state of relaxation, which is
drift away (associational flow
of ideas), or into a state of control, which is concentration.
Such a state is a habit for the
time being or, in other words,
the will has established a habit
of laxity or else of control
(nirodha).

The man who has learned
what concentration feels like,
can establish the state or mood

of concentration, which will then remain in force without his attention to it because it is a habit for the intended period. So one can be in the mood of concentration, or in the mood of spreading or drifting. This mood or habit-mold *(sanskāra)* will allow the habit of the flow of association of ideas (also called drift or spreading), or it will allow the habit of concentration or recall, as the case may be. In the former case the flow of thought is away from a center (which is the object of meditation), while in the latter case it is towards the center. Therefore in the latter case, as moment succeeds moment, the same object is repeated or revived. When the subsided and arisen images are similar in the successive moments there is a one-pointed condition of the mind. The habit-mold causes this to be a peaceful flow of concentration, which then continues without attention, as a foundation for meditation *(q.v.)* and contemplation *(q.v.),* or

complete *sanyama (q.v.).*

All the objects in the world, also the sense-organs in man have their habits, and these are subject to transformation (very slowly) from inside, because of their *sanskāras,* which includes a measure of repetitive dynamism or routine as well as static continuation.

Halāsana.
(The Plough Posture).

Lie on the back with the arms alongside, the palms on the ground. Raise the legs, and carry them over the head until the toes touch the floor. Raise the body up as much as possible and put the arms round the head on the ground.

Hansa. (Literally, a swan).

This is used as a symbol in various ways. As a title given to advanced yogīs it refers to the poetical belief that these birds fly for the monsoon season to Lake Mānasarovara, far up in the Himālaya Mountains, a place to which many of the most intrepid monks or *sanny-asīs (q.v.)* make their greatest pilgrimage, but the symbol is heightened by the fact that the highest *chakra (q.v.)* in man, or a portion of it, is also referred to as *mānasarovara.* There is also a poetical and mystical tradition that this bird is able to take and drink the milk out of a mixture of milk and water, and this accords with the idea that the wise yogī is able to extract the good out of all the mixed experiences of life.

In some schools the swan is called "the bird of time," a creature on the wing. This also accords with the condition of the wise yogī, who knows full well that in our material existence we are "on the wing," and it is not given to man to hold on to anything or to remain settled in one place or home permanently. He realizes that life is a book of changing and varied chapters and, adapting his mood of mind to this truth, he faces everything equ-

ably as it comes along, and uses it for the strengthening of his wings.

"Hare; like the horns of a".

A frequently used simile, to indicate that the object referred to does not exist, except in or by imagination or fancy. There are many other sayings, not so well known, similarly used, such as: "The furious elephant —tethered by the hair of a tortoise," and "The son of a barren woman."

Hari.

A name for Vishnu, indicating that he removes our sins or faults, from a verbal root which means "to take away." It is of course wisdom and love that remove sins or faults by the power of harmony which they contain, the great sin being selfishness or separateness, the source of all minor sins. Even the carnal sins are a violation of the harmony of the body, a kind of bodily selfishness in which the interest or excitement of a part overrides the welfare of the whole body.

Harmony.

One of the three divine powers, the other two being unity *(q.v.)* and variety *(q.v.)*. The best example of harmony is the human body, where we see all the organs and structures helping one another. In the mind it is love which, given intelligence in practical matters, could make a heaven on earth for the human family, because all would be in harmony, each contributing his or her ability and action.

Hatha-yoga.

A form of yoga which is concerned chiefly with the regulation of breathing, and secondarily with other bodily disciplines or training. Generally "ha" is taken to mean the action of inbreathing, and "tha" that of outbreathing, called respectively the sun and the moon breaths, and related by many commentators to the first two—*Prana* and *Apana*—of the five vital airs, or *Vāyus* *(q.v.)*. Hatha Yoga is widely considered to be an almost necessary prelude and assistant to Rāja-yoga, which is concerned with discipline of the mind. While it is true that the use of thought and especially the sedentary life usually disorders the natural processes of healthy breathing, for the purposes of Rāja-yoga—concentration, meditation, etc.—one need not undertake more discipline than to see that the breathing is quiet and orderly and to dissociate the mental efforts from any bodily effort or tension—in other words to take care that the good physical habit which has been set up or restored is not disturbed by the old error of thinking that physical sensation, effort or strain helps in meditation.

Head, Balance of the.

The head should always be well balanced on the neck

(q.v.). Its proper position can be established by imagining that it is being pulled up from above, like a puppet on a string —or, better, that we ourselves are pulling it up. A good practice also, formerly much recommended to boys and young men of Europe and America, was to remind oneself every now and then to press the neck back so as to feel the collar-stud at the back of the neck.

It is possible to "lift oneself by one's boot-straps." In yoga we do well to avoid too much of the idea that we are bound to the earth, even physically. When we are standing, the earth pulls us towards it by gravity, but we also pull it upwards to us, also by gravity. We thus have a share of the original power, and when walking or standing or sitting, we do to some extent float. Mentally, morally and spiritually we have a greater proportion of the original power, and a great influence upon our bod-

ies, which have their responses to these influences, which can be somewhat like the effect of setting into action the various lights and engines in a large factory room by the merest touch upon a small switch.

Healing.

This is carried on during sleep by the etheric double, as during that time there is little disturbance of it by personal thoughts and desires. As the harmony between the etheric double and the physical body then increases, the vital airs *(q.v.)* flow freely, and health is the result. There is, of course, no objection to the use of suitable medicines and remedies in aiding the physical body though healthy exercises (movements, stretchings relaxations, etc.) are most important, as otherwise the whole burden of healing is put on the etheric double, which is too much to ask, especially if, as very often occurs, it is being tormented by wrong and bad thoughts and emotions containing desires not in accordance with Nature.

In the matter of healing by the flow of life-force (vital air) from one person to another, this is usually automatic in the case of persons of pure mind and good will. The factor of intention applies in particular cases, but here it is to be remembered that no one can help much those who will not help themselves, and that those who are spoiling their bodies from the outside and their etheric doubles from the inside cannot hold well the life-force given by another. So at best one can only help the deserving, which occurs in many cases of convalescence, or at times of crises. It is good to lift the lame dog over the stile, but not to carry it all along the road. (See also under *vyana*).

The healing of the lower mind and the emotions is another matter, concerning the direct flow of telepathy from one to another, but here, too,

little can be done without a good background on the part of the "patient," so the best way in such transmissions is to run them on a current of imaginary conversation. In this it is to be remembered that familiar mental pictures are easiest to transmit. In this field mutual and collective meditations are beneficial, but should not be too much, if at all generally, directed from outside by the spoken word.

Hidden Treasure.

The lesson of hidden treasure is that this will not come out of the ground by simply calling it. We must have reliable information as to where it is, then remove the stones and dig.

Higher Mind, The.

That mind which is active, in thinking, loving or willing, or in gaining knowledge. In yoga terms it has the faculties of *manas, buddhi* and *ahankara* (q.v.). It is always concerned with some sort of harmony, as is seen in two ways: (1) in the gaining of knowledge it is discovering the harmonies in Nature, and (2) in planning or inventing it is fitting things together in harmony, so as to produce a combined effect. In this, it stands in contrast with the lower mind (q.v.).

Higher Self, The.

This is a modern term, but very convenient, for it reminds us that the purpose of life at the human stage is to feed, exercise and rest this higher self so that he may come to full stature. The law behind it is that by thinking, loving and willing in practical life the powers of thought, love and the will grow.

The business of *Rāja-yoga* is (1) to develop these three, especially by concentration, meditation and contemplation with reference to the things of incarnate experience, and (2) to let in the light of the spirit by

the pursuit of knowledge *(jnāna)* and devotion *(bhakti)* to it, remembering that the spirit can enter the picture in some degree at any stage on the journey, not only at the end of the road. Through the higher self that spirit can illuminate even the business of the lower self, and infuse all its doings with truth, goodness and beauty.

Householder, Yoga for the.

In India millions of people who do not devote themselves entirely to yoga obtain its benefit by selection of a portion for their own practice, to be done in spare time, or at some allotted time. The same can be done in other countries and if properly done should enable the doer to carry the burden and carry out the work of ordinary life with much more calmness and strength than before. This view is endorsed by the *Shiva Sanhitā,* from which the following extracts are taken.

"The practice should be done privately, avoiding company, and in seclusion. For the sake of the community ordinary outside matters should be carried on. All the proper duties of his own karmic status should be performed. When these are done without attachment there is no fault. The householder, wisely following this method will obtain success, without doubt. Remaining in the midst of the family, always doing the duties of the householder, free from sins and merits, with sense-desires controlled, he attains liberation. Doing his own proper actions, which are done for the welfare of mankind, he is not at fault (from the standpoint of yoga)."

I

Ichchhāshakti.

The power of the will, not merely over the thoughts and feelings in the mind—which is usual—but much further, so that desired events and occurrences and what some would call coincidences can be called into effect. It involves also the power to sustain and control the body in unusual ways, and is also behind the power of concentration which is used in *kriyāshakti (q.v.)*.

Idā.

A channel on the left of the *sushumnā (q.v.)*. This is described as coiling round the *sushumnā* and ending at the left nostril, or at the *ājnā chakra*.

Ignorance.

The root of all our troubles, *avidyā (q.v.)*.

Illusion.

The idea of anything as existing in its own right, without God; so if God is not seen nothing is correctly seen. One cannot think of a finger without a hand, or a tail without an animal. The severed finger is no finger. Similarly, anyone who thinks of a man without the God of which he is an appendage will be under an illusion. (See also under *Māyā*).

Imagination.

A most important faculty of the human mind, by which we can reproduce in the field of mental vision images of things previously sensed, and combinations of such things. Our thinking is then done in the mind, these images being moved about by our power of thought.

Incarnation.

This is due to desire for enjoyment of some kind. In the course of living these three follow in order: (1) perception, (2) enjoyment, (3) attainment. The last of these commonly passes unnoticed, as people are intent on enjoyments. But when something has been sufficiently enjoyed there arises the feeling of "enough" in reference to that thing, because the mind has achieved an attainment through it, as in the case of a child with a toy, or in the case of a joke, which becomes very stale when too often repeated.

The condition of the incarnation is, however, held to be provided by the law of karma *(q.v.)*, according to the deeds of the man in his earlier lives. It is really the condition of the man's mind—his emotions and thoughts—which has caused the actions which in turn have provided him with a certain kind of body, in a certain social milieu and with a certain financial status, etc. This is said to be like the action of a farmer who admits the irrigation water to certain channels, or closes it off, by opening or stopping the inlets, the flow of the water (or the karma) being something natural, but the direction of it having been provided for by the man.

It is held that certain advanced yogīs can take up more than one body, each having an artificial lower mind *(chitta)*, produced by meditation, which mind is, however, directed by the yogī's own higher mind, and so does not make any separate karma for itself. These carry on rather mechanically, but are available for the full presence or influence of the yogī whenever he chooses. By means of them he can deal with a greater variety of karma in one incarnation. This would involve advanced power of mind; the ordinary person has more than he can do to govern even one mind.

Individual, the.

An atom of life, or *jiva* (q.v.).

Indriyas, The ten.

These are the ten organs in the body by which the inner man gains knowledge of the world and uses it in the world. These are:

(1) Five sense-organs *(jnān-endriyas),* concerned with hearing, touching, seeing, tasting, and smelling, and

(2) Five action-organs *(kar-mendriyas)* concerned with walking, handling, speaking, procreation and evacuation.

It is in these ten that a human being mostly lives his bodily life. The sympathetic functions (see under vital airs) are simply a basis for these.

Intuition.

Whenever the power of one level has a reflection into it or an accompaniment of a higher which has, so to speak, come awake, there is what is called intuition. To take a very crude example, the driver of an automobile is an intuition to it, and takes it unerringly to the gasoline or petrol station to be refuelled. In man, the emotions direct the actions of the body; the knowledge in the lower mind directs (or should direct) the emotions; the higher thinking mind directs the lower mind; the love or ethical nature or wisdom directs the thinking into proper channels, and the uncontaminated will, with its own intuition of the self, will some day enlighten and direct the love. Intuitions may arise anywhere along this line, before the consciousness stands firmly, clearly and constantly in possession of the higher power or is fully illumined and unified with the intuitioner. Information brought in by dreams, telepathy, etc. often comes but is not strictly intuition.

Īshwara.

The divine willer. The supreme giver of what he has and is, which is liberty, and therefore that divine life which implants a portion of itself in every living being or *jīva (q.v.)*, which is then "the inner ruler, immortal." The notion that God rules or governs in the human sense, from the outside, is repugnant to the principle and aim of yoga, for such government (desirable as it may be in minor matters) involves restriction of individual choice and powers. It is the defect of harmony *(q.v.)* that it accepts a limitation of liberty, as love always does; but in the end harmony will be swallowed up in liberty when the yogī attains and lives in the power of unity, transcending human life and incarnation.

Īshwara-pranidhāna.
(Attentiveness to God).

One of the three practices for daily life and preliminary yoga prescribed by Patanjali. He also describes it as a noteworthy means to the attainment of the higher contemplation. It is a glad acceptance of the complete presence of God in all things and events.

J

Jāgrat.

The waking state. (See under Avasthās).

Japa. (Repetition).

This is not meditation, but is the repetition of an emotion or an idea, assisted by a word, for covering-up an undesired feeling or thought, and the establishment of a new habit in place of it. Many people repeat the words "Rām, Rām" when there is trouble; with some the thought then is that Rāma (considered as an expression of deity) may help, but with most the idea is to remember that the deity has the universe well in hand, so they may give up their distress. When japa is used, it may be done loudly or softly or merely mentally; the last is considered to be much the best and most effective.

Patanjali holds that when bad thoughts arise there should be reflection upon their contraries, this being defined as reflection upon the pain and error which arise from them. This is not repetition, nor is repetition meditation *(q.v.)*, but he does recommend repetition in one case, namely, in the use of the word "Om" *(q.v.)*, specifying, however, that this is to be with intentness on its meaning —which will advance.

Jāti.

One's status in the material world; one's immediate environment, including family conditions, social and economic status, etc. Every one's field of operations is necessarily small, but it is usually very definite. (See also under *Upādhi).*

Jīva or Jīvātma.

A living being. A unit of life. This, the core of our being, beyond body and mind, is our very self, our pure consciousness. One of the best known analogies for the relation between the individual and the divine is that of "the spark and the flame." This spark has "sparkness" and "flameness," and to speak of or meditate upon the "flameness of the spark" is to practice the highest yoga.

In popular speech the term simply distinguishes a living being of any kind from the non-living, lifeless (jada) or dead.

Jīvanmukti.

The state of being liberated while still embodied. The state of one who never while conscious loses sight of the ātmā; just as other persons are conscious of being the mind while they are using the body, the *Jīvanmukta* (one having *jīvanmukti)* is conscious of the *ātmā* while using the mind. This is not the same as mere thinking of the ātmā. The thinking is, however, a basis for the intuition of ātmā, and in no other matter is the injunction more true that when the intuition comes one must not be content with the intuition, but must rise to the intuitioner.

K

Kaivalya. (Independence).

This is the god-like state, in which the pure consciousness of the real man is not affected by the afflictions and lures of the world and the mind. It is liberation. It arises when the purity of the intelligence of the mind is so perfected that it is not stained, prejudiced or lured by anything, and is, as it were, equal to the purity of the pure untainted consciousness or real man (*purusha*). At last the man will stand forth in the full light and power of unobstructed consciousness, without the need of world, or body, or mind.

Kāma. (Desire, or emotion).

Memories of pleasures and pains previously experienced in connection with various objects arise as feelings of liking and disliking when those objects are brought into view in fact and in thought, and these engender emotions of desire and aversion. These *kāmas*, when thus spontaneous, are regarded as part of our kārmic heritage (see Karma, law of), but they can be changed by the present intelligence and will of the man who has them, and new habits and connections can be formed. The emotions are in this sense external to the man—something that he *has,* not that he does or is—being similar to the body in this respect. They should never be mistaken for the man himself.

Desire or emotion is not to be crushed out, but to be strengthened, purified and used selectively. The two *undesirable* departments of emotion and desire are mentioned in the *Bhagavad Gītā* under the names *bhoga* (sensuous enjoyments) and *aishwarya* (the enjoyment of personal self-satisfaction), and the same book speaks of *kāma* as divine when it is not contrary to *dharma,* which is the proper way of life, worthy of a human being destined by his own efforts to have union with God and thus to receive that grace and consciously share that nature.

Kārana. (See under Upadhis).

Karma. (Literally, action or doing).

Any action is called a karma, provided there is initiative or intention in the act. Thus when a carpenter makes a chair we call it his action, but if a flag waves in the breeze we do not say it acts, but only that it moves. So the term might be better explained as "doing," rather than "action." The term is used also to indicate the law of karma *(q.v.)* by which every individual reaps the reward of his own efforts and actions, both good and bad.

Karma, the Law of.

The idea that everything is paid for in the same coinage—give affection and you will be repaid by affection; give thought and you will be repaid by knowledge; give labour and you will be repaid by goods, and so on, with respect to all giving and taking, all kindness and unkindness, all good or evil conduct, emotion or thought. It is implied also that what we now receive is the result of our past actions, etc.— what you work for you have; what you have stolen you lose.

Karma is of three kinds:

what one is now making *(kri-yamāna* or *vartamāna),* what one is now receiving, or what from the past is now fructifying *(prārabdha),* and what one has in storage *(sanchita)* for the future. In the case of ordinary people karma is also called white, black and mixed, meaning pleasant, painful and mixed; white being the result of intelligence, goodness and self-control. Yogīs, however, who have reached the point of regarding all fructifying karmas as equal (through practical discrimination of their usefulness as means of experience and purification or development) are thereby said to have karma which is neither black nor white. They do not guide their lives by considerations of pleasure and pain. Further, by treating present karmas with *vairāgya (q.v.)* they do not have the desires which modify them into future karmas.

Some karmas are in suspension or storage because all the various results of past actions or doings cannot be expressed all at once in one set or type of life and environment, but some are obstructed by present conditions and are therefore latent or suspended. They will manifest when suitable opportunities occur. It is to be understood that "what has gone" and "what has not yet come" are realities in nature, and are therefore potencies, but—this is emphatic—they have their own kind of reality, which is not the same as that of what exists at the present time. In the mind, memory and reason open the doors for their influence in the present. Both the kinds of latent potencies have characters of the qualities *(gunas, q.v.)* of Nature, just as present objects have. There is objective reality of actions and their results, in the yoga philosophy.

Although the karma which has fructified or begun its operation cannot be annulled, but must be dealt with, this is not the case with the stored karma;

thus, *e.g.*, an act of kindness in the present will cancel out an act of unkindness done in the past.

Karma has reference to actions and facts, not to the operational powers of the higher self—thus love, *e.g.*, does not make karma, but loving actions do. An injury done by A to B may be returned from C. But love is a force of attraction, and when people love one another personally they will come together again regardless of circumstances or karmas, it being beyond the material law and a direct operation and relationship of the higher selves.

Karma-yoga.

The yoga of or by action. Action or business in the world is not in itself a form of yoga, for it may be motivated by selfishness of the comfort-and-sensuous kind or of the self-satisfaction kind, but if it is carried on unselfishly with a view to the welfare of others or the "welfare of the world" *(loka-sangraha, q.v.),* then it is karma-yoga. The industrialist or business man who takes into account the welfare of his customers, his employees, his associates, and indeed all whom he deals with or meets in the course of his commerce is a *karma-yogī.* It was said of some men of great wealth and influence that they regarded themselves not as the proprietors but as the trustees of their riches. The same idea applies to all walks of life, at every level, and whether the contacts be few or many or small or great. It is thus open to everyone who can be at all unselfish to be sometimes and to some extent a *karma-yogī,* but not when there is merely selfishness at second-hand or *egoism-à-deux,* which is the case where there is infatuation or favoritism.

The subject of *karma-yoga* is especially expounded in the *Bhagavad-Gītā.* In that teaching it is seen to be action motivated by *buddhi (q.v.),* that is, knowledge and love of the life-side, the mind and soul of one's co-beings.

Kleshas, The Five.

The five sources of trouble, which are *avidyā* (ignorance), *asmitā* (self-personality), *rāga* (desire), *dwesha* (aversion), *abhinivesha* (possessiveness). They are all due to the first of them, namely, error or mistaken ideas. They can be, at different times, dormant, slight, obstructed or vigorous. They are weakened by *kriyā-yoga* (daily-life virtues) and destroyed by *dhyāna* (meditation). They are the root-cause of embodiment, and its status and conditions, with their pleasures and pains, resulting from past virtues and vices, or merits and demerits.

Knower, Knowing & Known. (Jnātri, Jnāna, Jneya).

It will some time be realized in the course of progress in *jnāna-yoga* that the knower knowing something that is known consists of only one reality, not three. It is easy to argue that in the realization of the one Brahman or Ātmā "without a second" this must perforce be so, but the same truth is found in the mind, when introspection shows us that the knowing is the knower — not that there is some being not of the nature of knowing, who does acts of knowing— and also that the known is also the knower, inasmuch as the known is all karma, and is an outpost or expression of the knower—as in the case of an artist looking at one of his own pictures, and thereby seeing himself, since his work, like a mirror, tells what he is. So in the end it is seen that there is only knowing, knowing, knowing.

Knowledge, bases of.

These are three: perception (*pratyaksha*), inference (*anumāna*), and reliable testimony (*āgama*). Intuition is an inner perception.

Koan.

A term used in Zen Buddhism. A *koan* is a mind-baffling statement to be meditated upon. The teacher who propounds it requires an answer; he is in no hurry for it, but the student is expected to keep to the task until he has a solution, although the statement is such that there is no intellectual solution possible. Such a statement is: "The two hands clap with a noise; listen to the clap of one hand." Reason cannot give an answer, cannot even try to do so, but as the student perseveres and there is no reasoning, the steam, so to speak, which could not get out in one way breaks through in another, and there comes an intuition (*satori*), which suddenly appears, a lighting-up of the mind which probably causes an involuntary exclamation or action.

This method is somewhat akin to the pursuit of thought on any abstract subject to the point where it becomes paradoxical, as in the attempts to reconcile the infinity of time and space with units of the same, or the attempts to square the circle, or find the area of a disc, in square measure, which just cannot be done.

Koshas.

A *kosha* is a vessel in which something is stored or contained, and is often thought of in terms of a sword and its scabbard or sheath. Man is described as having five *koshas,* as follows:

1. *Annamayakosha.* Literally, the vessel or sheath composed of food—the dense physical body.

2. *Prānamayakosha.* Literally, the vessel or sheath composed of *prāna* (*q.v.*).

3. *Manomayakosha.* Literally, the vessel or sheath composed of *prāna* (*q.v.*).

mind, both higher and lower, which includes *manas, chitta,* and *kāma (q.v.).*

4. *Vijnānamayakosha.* Literally, the vessel or sheath composed of wisdom (the *buddhi, q.v.).*

5. *Ānandamayakosha.* Literally the vessel or sheath composed of joy. (Vedantically speaking, the *ahankāra,* the living being's self-expression of Unity).

These five sheaths are classified along with the three *sharīras (q.v.)* or *dehas,* or *upādhis, (q.v.)* as follows:

Kārana-upādhi (q.v.) contains *Ānandamayakosha.*

Sūkshma-upādhi (q.v.) comprises *Vijnānamayakosha, Manomayakosha,* and *Prānamayakosha.*

Sthūla-upādhi (q.v.) contains *Annamayakosha.*

Krikala.

One of the minor vital airs *(q.v.).*

Krishna, Shrī.

A great king reputed to have lived in India about five thousand years ago as a divine incarnation come to turn the world into new and better ways of living, as the divine is considered to do from time to time when necessary. His teaching to his devotee Arjuna forms the famous work entitled the *Bhagavad Gītā (q.v.).* An emphatic part of his message was the doctrine that every man can reach the divine by doing his own duty to his fellow men with their welfare in view, which is the *buddhi-yoga (q.v.).*

Kriyāshakti.

This is literally the power of action, but it means the action of the mind, which is thought. Thought is behind all our actions except such as are reflex, and also with regard to these indirectly, since their forms and habits result from mind-action in the past. *Kriyāshakti* is power of thought over matter in a degree altogether beyond its normal action in influencing the especially adapted and responsive centers in the body which make our bodily action possible and easy, so much so that in fact its employment would produce material results looking like small miracles, though of course in every case the whole procedure would be well within the field of nature and natural law. It depends primarily upon great power of concentration of mind.

Kriyā-yoga.
The yoga of action.

Stated by Patanjali to have three departments: *tapas* (bodily self-government), *swādhyāya* (mental study), *īshwara-pranidhāna* (an emotional attitude of attentiveness to God), and therefore meaning the the yoga for daily life, in contrast to that prescribed for the time given to meditation. It is regarded by some as the pre-liminary or preparatory yoga, to be done to some extent before taking up systematic meditation, but anyhow to continue always, governing the conduct of life. As such it is a help towards meditation and in reducing the five causes of trouble (*kleshas*) which beset human life.

Kshetrajna.

Knower of the field (*kshetra*) or body. The body is the field of operations for the lord or master of the body, who is the self within, while the body is made up of eight forms of matter, five of which are objective—namely earth, water, fire, air and ether— and three of which are subjective— namely *manas, buddhi* and *ahankāra* (*q.v.*). The *Garbha Upanishad* states that through *buddhi* one knows and evaluates, through *manas* one thinks and fancies, through *chitta* one recognizes and recollects, and through *ahankāra* one feels as "I."

Kukkutāsana.
(The Cock Posture).

The body is held off the ground, standing on two legs (as it were) formed by the hands being put down between the thighs and the knees, the legs being folded as in *padmāsana*.

Kumbhaka.
(Literally, as a pot).

The retention of breath in *prānāyāma* (*q.v.*).

Kundalinī.

A force described as lying coiled up like a serpent—in three coils—in a cavity near the base of the spine. It is always spoken of as a goddess— a fundamental power or force —and therefore as "she." She lies there normally with her head blocking a fine channel which goes straight up the spine and is called *sushumnā* (*q.v.*). In the practice of *laya-yoga* (*q.v.*), she is awakened, and proceeds up the channel, on which six *chakras* (*q.v.*) are threaded. Some yogīs have described this process as accompanied by a feeling of warmth moving up the spine. Each *chakra* on being vitalized by her is "alerted," and there will then be some enhanced sensation and power, according to the "principle" of the human being to which the given *chakra* is related. It is, of course, eminently important not to alert the lower *chakras* until one has full or at least great control of and power over one's body and emotions.

External methods of awakening the *kundulinī* are described in some of the *hatha-yoga* books, but the would-be yogī is in those books advised never to try them except under the direct supervision of a competent teacher. In that case, *āsanas, kumbhakas* and *mudrās* (*q.v.*) can all be used. Strict *rāja-yogīs* avoid such methods altogether, knowing that *kundalinī* will gradually awaken naturally as their meditations proceed, in most cases without being noticed at all.

The literature describing the tour of the *chakras* which is made by the *kundalinī* is poetical rather than literally descriptive. In the spinal channel called *sushumnā*, there is one still finer called *vajroli*, and within that still another called *chitrinī*, described as "fine as a spider's web." The yogī brings the *kundalinī* as far as he can, and as she goes through any of the lotuses or *chakras* its face, which was previously turned downwards, turns upwards. As she leaves each *chakra* or *padma* on the way up she withdraws the functions of that center, and so makes them latent, until she reaches the "thousand-petalled lotus" at the top of the head, beyond all the six *chakras,* and there enjoys enhanced life, so that on the return journey she can give back to each *chakra* its own specific powers, purified and enhanced. This may awaken some degree of clairvoyance and similar powers, but what the yogī sees will depend on his state of mind, and even then his interpretation and understanding will depend on his evolutionary status and his ability to eliminate "the personal factor" with reference to what he sees.

Kūrma.

One of the minor vital airs. (*q.v.*).

Kūtastha.

What stands above or beyond illusion. The *ātmā* or true "I" in man. In the *Bhagavad Gītā* he is described as *kūtastha* who is satisfied with knowledge and experience, has mastered the senses, and regards equally a lump of earth, or a rock or gold, especially if he is also the same towards well-wishers, friends, enemies, strangers, neutrals, haters, kinsmen, saints and sinners.

Kūthastha. (Literally, standing at the top).

A term applied to the Self, which is unchanging, above the changing phenomena of the world, both objective and subjective. As in a genealogical table the person who appears at the head of it is termed *kūtastha,* the meaning is clear. The aboveness of the yogī who is one with the spiritual self, or is truly himself is further seen by the example of the blacksmith's anvil (*kūta*) on which many forms are hammered out without modification of the anvil itself.

L

Lamp, The Steady.

This simile is applied especially to the yogī who is engaged in *ātmā-yoga* (*q.v.*). He is steady: "just as a lamp standing where there is no wind does not flicker."

Law, the Great.

In modern times a term preferred by Buddhists to the word God. It is a translation of *dhamma* (or *dharma, q.v.*), the right way of living, which is indicated in the Noble Eightfold Path *(q.v.)* as the only way to release from suffering and sorrow. It is universal and unchangeable and to be obeyed. Law is also the greatest blessing for man, for did it not exist in the world, or could it be fanciful or capricious, there would be an end to human reason, love and the will. It is thus the very goodness permeating the world, and touching us at all points and times. If the world presents opposition to our desires and faculties, there too the goodness of the law is seen, for had these difficulties not been faced by us we should not be where we now are and what we now are. Had they been too great for us we would have been overwhelmed and exterminated; had they been too little we would now be much less advanced. So in the relationship between man and the world the Great Law is again revealed, in its character of the greatest Wisdom and the greatest Friend. Even our faults are included in the Law, for, as a poet once put it: "Blindly the wicked work the righteous will of Heaven."

Laws.

There are laws of Nature and laws of Life which no man can set aside, or can flout without becoming a cripple or insane, or dead in body or soul. In the former class we find the laws of established relationships between matters and forces in the field of science and the laws of health for the body, emotions and lower mind. In the latter are the spiritual laws—that the powers of the mind (will, love and thought) grow only by exercise, and that the pilgrimage of the *jīva (q.v.)* must end in

liberation *(q.v.)* or *nirvāna.* Since men in general are advancing by obedience to the *Law* and profiting by their increasing knowledge of it, we may expect future races of humanity to be composed of god-men, where at present we have men-men (all too few), animal men, vegetable-men and even mineral-men, among the last three of whom there is a good deal of animalating, vegetating and mineraling, and but little man-ing.

Laya-Yoga.

That system of yoga in which the chief emphasis is laid upon awakening and directing the latent force of the *kundalinī (q.v.)* which normally sleeps at the base of the spine. Closely linked with this are the religious treatises called *Tantras,* which contain mystical formularies for working with the powers pictured as gods and goddesses which have their functions in the universe

85

or macrocosm with equivalents or corresponding centers of power in the microcosm of the human form, especially in connection with *kundalinī* and the *chakras* (*q.v.*).

Levitation.

Walking over water, over thorns, etc. without contact, or simply rising and remaining suspended for a while. Patanjali declares this to be done by mastery over one of the vital airs, named *udāna* (see Vital Airs). It is mastered by *sanyama* (*q.v.*) on it.

Liberation. (Moksha).

The release of the spirit from connection with limited or manifest existence, hence also the cessation of its round of births and deaths. The Buddhist term is *nirvāna* (*q.v.*). Patanjali's term is *kaivalya* (*q.v.*).

As ignorance (*avidyā, q.v.*) is the cause of the conditioned existence, it disappears—as the contents of a dream do on awakening—when there arises the knowledge or illumination which involves release. This is the final and spiritual attainment for which human beings are destined, but it will not occur automatically, because the human being is positive.

Light, the Inner.

When one recalls to mind some facts of experience in order to dwell upon them or reconsider them, they are often seen in the inner light of the mind. This light belongs to the mind, and it is with this light belonging to the mind that the yogī may see things in the astral light, as the objective vision of the subtle effects of the mind (whether of thought or emotion) is called. The light of our physical seeing—not the same as the mere vibrations or transmissions of light as studied by the physicist —is the same when there is sight, so that seeing is always accompanied by some degree and kind or recognition, and is mental. The inner light of the mind is the third degree of separation or manifestation, and involves knowing without being. It may be compared with the inner touch, which is the second degree of separate knowing. It is a matter of frequent experience that a yogī will know by the inner touch the presence of a Teacher or other higher denizen of the astral light. It may be compared also with the inner sound (q.v.) which could be called the first veil, if the reader will understand that all manifest or separate or objective knowing is by the power of veils, and involves some exclusion or inhibition of full knowing.

Light, the (Prakāsha).

Always means the inner light of the mind, which is intuition from the personal point of view.

Linga Sharira, The.

The subtle body (*sukshma sharīra,* or *upādhi q.v.*), but sometimes only that part of it which is called the etheric double (*q.v.*).

Loka-sangraha.
(The welfare of the world).

Literally this means the harmonious combination of the people in any given locality or habitat. The idea is extended to include not merely their material welfare, but also all that pertains to their psychological welfare, (emotionally, mentally and ethically) or growth, individual and collective.

Lokas, The.

Lokas are habitats or regions or levels of existence of living beings. Thus there is the physical world within the range of our senses, which is called *bhūrloka.* Next in the invisible or subtle world, comes *bhuvarloka,* and then *swarloka.* It is in these regions that the yogī who has become master of his emotions and thoughts can when he wishes travel in his subtle body, which is then especially adapted to this purpose. The third of these regions is usually identified with the material heaven world to which ordinary good people are believed to go after death, to enjoy a glorified earth-life and to remain until their store of good is exhausted, after which they return to earth incarnation.

Love.

The power of harmony (*q. v.*), seen in human life as love.

Lower Mind, The.

That mind which collects, stores and remembers the information obtained through the senses, and thoughts concerning them. Through the association of ideas it is active in a drifting sort of way, though the drift from one idea to another is governed by certain laws or habits, which can be called the four roads of thought, which show how the lower mind is not a jungle but is a garden with well-marked paths or a state well provided with main roads to facilitate communications. The four roads are (1) the relation of genus and species, or class and particulars, including that between members of the same class, and including contrasts also (which, we must notice, are only between members of the same class), (2) the relation of part and whole, (3) the relation of a quality and that which has it, and (4) the relation by juxtaposition in either familiar or emphatic experience. In thinking of a rose, *e.g.* the following might come up along the four roads: (1) wild roses, garden roses with various names, other flowers, (2) petals, stamens, rose-bush, (3) color, scent, (4) roses particularly known, flower-vase, etc. In the drift, the relation is always concerning a pair, so that this mind walks as it were on two legs, or on stepping stones, as, *e.g.* in the flow: rose - garden - house - bedroom - sleep-dream-etc., in which on reaching "house" one drops "rose." In yoga, it is one of the chief practices to replace this habitual drift by an ability to concentrate, to be used whenever desired, so that before leaving the rose one may then consider all that it has to offer.

In the lower mind also there is the attachment of feelings of various kinds of liking and disliking to objects and thoughts and out of these arise many forms of emotional excitement and impulsiveness—which also are to be studied and dealt with in the pursuit of yoga.

Lower Self, The.

This is a modern term, but very useful if properly understood, for by making it orderly and harmonious with the laws of Nature, one can have a personal condition which puts no obstacle in the way of *rāja-yoga*. First, it should be known to have three parts—the physical, the emotional and the lower mental. In a sense all three are material, and can all be called bodies, inasmuch as they constitute three organisms having fixed or habitual reactions and instinctive actions resulting from the past. Next, each of these three must be put into orderly or healthy condition, which means the overcoming of laziness and sluggishness and the development of strength and energy, and then the ordering of those energies (never the suppression) into a good pattern, so that there will be strength with order, all in proper proportion. Strength with order is health, and provides for peace with activity.

In addition to all this, this triple lower self should be so equipped physically, emotionally and mentally, as to fit well into its environment.

Time given by the higher

self to the governing and equipping of this lower self is not wasted, for there is much development of will, affection and thought-power in the doing of it, and besides, there is a saving of time and energy in the long run even in the business of attention to material affairs.

M

Macrocosm.

The collective or universal world, as compared with the microcosm, which is the small world of a human being. Corresponding to the three *upādhis* *(q.v.)* of the latter are the three states of the macrocosm named the *avyakta* (literally, unmanifest), the *hiranyagarbha* (literally, the golden germ—a name of Vishnu), and *virāt* (the material world or manifestation).

Mahābhārata.

One of the two great epic poems of ancient India, the other being the *Rāmāyana*. The *Mahābhārata* is especially notable as it contains the famous scripture of Yoga, the *Bhagavad Gītā (q.v.)*. Both these classics are filled with references to the yogic way of life.

Mahābhūtas.

The five material elements *(q.v.)* or states of matter. Our "chemical elements" are not these, but are compounded forms. (See *Elements).*

Mahātmās.
(Literally, Great Souls).

A name popularly given to human beings who are highly developed. In the *Bhagavad Gītā* it refers to those who are constantly consciously aware of the omnipresence of the divine.

Maheshwara.

The great god, Shiva *(q.v.)*.

Manas.

The instrument of action in the mind or internal organ *(antahkarana, q.v.)*, which produces and modifies objective things. It is the thinking power or function which, in man, acts mainly through his body, and only in a lesser degree in an indefinite manner through telepathy, etc., unless it is well developed or well trained, or is intensely excited. As there are so many people thinking generally in a drifting or a disorderly manner, there is a considerable psychic atmosphere produced by this. (See under *Telepathy).*

Manipūraka Chakra, The.

The wheel or lotus at the level of the navel. It has ten petals of a green or a cloud-like color, bearing the letters d (cerebral), dh (cerebral), n (cerebral), t (dental), th (dental), d (dental), dh (dental), n (dental), p and ph. The animal shown in this case is a ram, which may be considered of a more fiery temperament than the elephant or the dolphin *(makara),* and so be appropriate to the objective mind, eager to get at, know and use external objects. The *bīja mantra* in this chakra is *ram,* in a fiery triangle having a *swastika* on each side. The devotion in this case will be connected with Brahmā, but it will be especially the thought aspect of Brahmā which appears in the human mind, in the lower stages as planning to obtain material things and in the higher stages as creative activity (see also *kriyāshakti).* (There are differences of opinion as to the placing of the deities in the various chakras, but these are not fundamental and do not involve a conflict of opinion, as there are wheels within wheels in this matter, and each *guru* or teacher follows a specific course suited to his system and his pupils). (See also under *Mūlādhāra* and *Chakras*).

Manomayakosha.
(See under Kosha).

Mantras.

Forms of speech which carry a material effect upon the mind, emotions or body, or even on things. The idea that suitable words and sentences can be effective in this manner is based upon the belief that all motion is accompanied by sound, though many of the motions in Nature may give sound beyond the range of human ears. More than this, such sounds are really words or announcements, the meaning of which could be read by one who knows—in which case there would be perfect communication or "language." Still more (and in accordance with the fact that in the natural world function precedes struc-ture) an idea precedes the spoken word, which in turn is creative.

All the sounds made and words used by human beings carry an influence of mind over matter. If these are arranged by some person competent in this matter, words of power and sentences of power can be formed. Such a person was called a mantramaker *(mantrakāra)* in ancient India. The scriptures contain many great *mantras,* of which the greatest is the word *Om (q.v.).* (See also *Gayatri, Shānti,* and *Tat-twamasi).*

Matha.

A monastery, where people can practice yoga without outside disturbance, and generally with the aid, if required, of other students or, more strictly, monks or persons dedicated at least for the time being to the pursuit of religion or yoga. It is usually recommended to be established in a place where the earth is good, not on rocks, and which is not damp, nor subject to earthquakes and volcanoes, and it should also be under a virtuous and uninterfering government or king. If it is a private "meditation room" that is being considered, the old specifications — not, however, rigid — recommend that it be medium sized and level, have only one opening— the doorway, which should be small—and clean. It should have a little courtyard, surrounded by a wall. In the courtyard there should be a well and a seat.

Mauna.

Silence, in the sense of abstaining from speech. It is always considered advisable not to talk about one's practice of yoga, partly because it is an indication that one is more interested in the talk than in the yoga, and partly because there may be a little interference with one's meditation arising from the curiosity of other people, whose thought-forms can come

along telepathically. One who deliberately practices silence is called a *muni (q.v.).*

Mauna is also that silence which necessarily occurs in the case of knowledge or experience so deep that it cannot be spoken of, because in ordinary experience of both body and mind there is nothing to compare with it.

Māyā.

Often translated "illusion." The doctrine that all that is experienced in the manifested universe is illusion. This is not, however to be confused with "delusion," for in the latter case there would be nothing there, but in the former there is something — the Reality — but we are seeing it wrongly.

Māyā has two functions: covering-up *(āvarana)* and throwing-out *(vikshepa).* The first is like a veil, which hides something, so that in the manifested world there is an absence of something which we may say exists in the divine world. The second is the business that goes on when the mind gets active among what is available or what is left after the *āvarana* has done its veiling of the reality. There is, of course, a good deal of this activity which contains but little intelligence, but as time goes on there is more and more creation of orderly and harmonious objects or forms. Still, at best, in the orderliness as well as in the turbulence and the turgidness, there is "illusion" which the consciousness must overcome before it can be liberated from bondage to the subjective and objective world.

There is, of course nothing but the Reality, but when the most of it is concealed by veils, like a lady's face, if it were covered by several meshes one over the other in turn but little of the Reality is seen, yet what is seen is still the same Reality—the same face. Hence the illusion is due to our inability to pierce the veils, mainly because our desires lie on this side of them, but it is never total illusion.

The adjective "indescribable" *(anirvachanīya)* is often applied to the idea of *māyā;* it means that it cannot properly be described as either real or unreal, since a *māyā* in the field of *māyā* is relatively real, though the whole field of *māyā* (or separation or relativity) is not real but is only the collectivity of the māyās. Metaphysically, any object can only be fully, that is correctly, known even mentally in comparison with and in relation to everything else, and its cause is everything, including itself, in which last thought its reality is found. On this account, the unreal can serve to awaken us to the real, like a snake *(q.v.)* in a dream.

Mayūrāsana.
(The Peacock Posture).

The body is balanced horizontally above the ground, on the elbows, the palms of the hands being on the ground. Usually the legs are folded as in padmāsana.

Meditation. (Dhyāna).

Is a continuous mental effort with respect to a chosen object or topic. It should be a complete flow of one's thought, having the basic character of concentration — the effort of concentration having been forgotten but remaining as an established mood of the will for the period. A complete flow of thought implies that all the related ideas that one can find in the mind are brought together. A systematic series of mental associations or "roads of thought" may be used if desired, in which case one will formulate and answer questions such as the following: (1) With reference to comparison, what are the other objects of the same kind or class, and in what respects do they agree with and differ from this object? (2) What are the parts of the object and what functions do they perform in it, and of what larger object is this a part? (3) What are the qualities of the object, how are they related to one another and the whole, and of what larger object is this a quality? (4) What notable actual experience or thought have I had with respect to the mere association of this with other objects, whether in seeing, hearing, or thought?

The practice of meditation may begin with simple concrete objects, then complex concrete, then simple abstract, then complex abstract.

Meditation tidies up the mind, which is usually full of disorder, and lubricates it, as it were, so that when this power of the mind is set in action there is easily a fountain of thoughts. When fully successful it removes all confusion and conflict from the mind, preparing it for new mental perceptions and the reception of intuitions. It also increases the *grasp* of the mind, by enlarging the content of the *grip* which is attained by the practice of concentration.

Memories. (Smritis).

One group or class of the ideas *(vritti, q.v.)* which rise in the lower mind *(chitta);* those which reproduce some scenes or thoughts from the past.

Merudanda.

Another term for the spine, but full of symbology, since in the old stories all the things of the world were produced from an ocean of milk in which the mountain named Meru stood. With the middle of the great serpent of eternity or time wound round the mountain, the gods and demons, pulling at either end, churned the ocean by the turning of the mountain as a stick. *Danda* means a stick.

Microcosm.
(See under Macrocosm).

Mind, Evenness of.
(See under Samatwa).

Mind, purity of, means to.

Patanjali gives several means to purity of mind, which is clearness of mind *(chitta-pra-sāda)*, as follows:

1. By cultivation of friendliness to those who are happy,
   sympathy to those who are suffering,
   gladness at the sight of the good,
   and disregard of the bad.
2. By taking some long breaths.

Mind, Steadiness of.

Patanjali states that this can be attained in several ways, as follows:

(1) When there is or has been some reliable occult experience of one's own, or when there is cultivated increase of higher sensitivity (including telepathy, clairvoyance, clairaudience, psychometry, intuition, etc.) there arises a settled and confident condition of the mind. The active thinking mind is indicated here by the word

manas, which is distinct from the lower mind, which stores ideas and has the mechanical flow of the association of ideas, which is called *chitta.*

(2) Or, by the rise of a peaceful inner light. Many people on shutting the eyes see an inner light, which gives a sense of peace and of confidence. Sometimes, in this light pictures, at first casual but very clear and beautiful, may arise. Sometimes, *e.g.* as taught by the ancient teacher Vāchaspati Mishra, one may find this light by poising one's consciousness in the region of the heart. Here one may see thought-forms, he tells us. The *manas* itself is the inner light in which forms appear.

(3) Or, the lower mind (*chitta*) may picture persons or beings, such as saints and adepts, who have attained freedom from desires.

(4) Or, when there is dwelling upon experiences of dream and sleep.

(5) Or, by meditation upon anything in which one may be specially interested.

Mind-Poise, The.
(Sanyama, q.v.).

This is the action of the mind in its attention to any thing or idea when all its powers are as it were gathered together and directed to that thing or idea. It begins with concentration and culminates in contemplation *(q.v.).*

Mithyā.

The falsity which has to be seen through, or overcome, for the attainment of liberation or the realization of the true Self.

Moha.

Confusion and foolishness, with their companion, sorrow *(shoka)*—all due to ignorance of the facts of life, as found in the science and philosophy of life.

Moksha. (Liberation).

The final and spiritual attainment of the human being; the goal of human life; *nirvāna* *(q.v.); kaivalya (q.v.).*

Mondo.

A term used in Zen Buddhism. It means a sudden question asked by the teacher, to which the student must give an immediate reply, without thought, although the question has been so framed that there is no logical answer. The student's spontaneous answer may be no more than an exclamation, but the alertness of the mind, without content, should bring some new experience.

Mortification.

This is not countenanced by any of the classical standard works on either rāja-yoga or hatha-yoga. On the contrary, excellence and perfection of body are often extolled (See under *Body, Perfection of*).

Motion.

Space, time and motion are three facts of being which every yogī has to take into account. He finds a place (space) for his meditation, which should be small, secluded, level, and free from damp, insects and wind, or else, it may be under a tree where not too many people pass near. Many people engaged in regular occupations most of the day have in their homes special rooms devoted solely to this purpose. Then there is a time to be allotted, and also it is to be remembered that every act of the mind, every logical process, takes time, for, while material objects have extensity or "occupy space," mental acts extend in time. The third fact is motion or change, which takes place both in the world and in the mind, on account of the play of the powers of space and time. Visible motion is thus, say the symbologists, the result of two forces acting at right angles to each other, having such a balance to each other that their impact or coalescence produces circular motion —a form very commonly seen in Nature. What seems circular is, however, not completely so, for there is always a difference, however slight, when the movement reaches again its initial phase, so that we must regard the motion as spiral rather than circular.

Mudrās.

These are various physical practices of *hatha-yoga* variously listed from ten to twenty-five in number, used to some extent for health but chiefly for obtaining psychic powers and experience, including the awakening of *kundalinī* (*q.v.*). Most of them are very dangerous, and should be tried only under the direct supervision of a teacher. From the standpoint of *rāja-yoga* they are quite unnecessary. To give a general idea of them we list a few of the best known:—

Khechari-mudrā. The tongue is gradually lengthened over a period of six months. It can then be turned upwards into the cavity at the back of the palate. Then, with breath sus-

pended entirely, and sometimes with other bodily entrances closed with oiled cotton pads, the yogī may remain in trance without breathing for perhaps forty days or longer. Several test cases of this kind are on record.

Uddīyāna-bandha. The contraction of the abdominal muscles so as to press the intestines upwards and towards the spine. This is good for strengthening those muscles and teaching them the good habit of keeping the abdomen in. It can therefore be practiced by modern sedentary persons with great advantage—say a hundred times up and down once or twice a day. The exercise should stop in the up position, as there should be no *voluntary* adoption of the down position. Deep breathing exercises of a simple kind can be done with advantage while holding the up position, but should be done with a conscious expansion of the muscles concerned, not by mere intake of breath. This *mudrā* is considered to be pre-eminently beneficial in the retention of youthfulness. The exercise may be varied by drawing up at each side of the center, not only centrally up.

Viparītakaranī. Lie on the back with the head on the ground and hands at first on the ground. Raise the legs up in the air. Raise also the lower part of the back, supporting it now with the hands, while the elbows remain on the ground and take the weight. The legs may be moved round and round a little.

Pāsinīmudrā. The legs are wrapped round the neck, like a noose *(pāsha).*

Kākī-mudrā. Contract the lips to resemble the beak of a crow *(kaka)* and suck air in very slowly.

Mātangīnī-mudrā. This is called the elephant-*mudrā,* because elephants like to stand in water, take it up in their trunks and throw it out again, often on their own backs. Stand neck-deep in water. Drink some in through the nostrils, and send it out through the mouth. Then draw water in by the mouth and send it out through the nostrils.

Mūlādhāra Chakra, The.

The wheel or lotus at the base of the spine, on a level about half-way between the anus and the sexual organs. It has four petals of a red color, bearing the letters v, sh (palatal), sh (cerebral) and s. In the centre of the *chakra* is a fiery triangle (containing the coiled-up *kundalinī)* inside a yellow square, which indicates the material principle called earth, and often there is also a picture of an elephant to indicate strength or stability — the power of extensity which the earth has, to keep its three-dimensional form. The *bīja* (seed) *mantra (q.v.)* connected with this element is *lam.* This is the general sound, the letters of the petals being modifications in it.

If there is meditation *on* a *chakra*—i.e. on the symbols its picture contains—or *in* a *chakra,* there should always be deep devotion with intention to serve the purposes of one or other of the three great divine powers represented by Shiva, Vishnu or Brahmā which ramify into all things. This service may have reference to external things, purposes and actions, or it may be concerned with efforts of the inner man to realize and express to the full the powers of his own being. In the present case, as Brahmā can be divided into three, it is the will aspect of Brahmā which is predominant, though all three of the lower *chakras* (this and *swādhishthana* and *manipūraka)* are *basically* under the influence of the Brahmā power, which can, of course, present three modifications of itself, connected with *tamas* and the will, *rajas* and desire, *sattwa* and intelligent order, respectively. Reverence for the Brahmā power means in the

lower stages, proneness to material temptations, and, in the higher stages of human life, intelligent valuation and use of material things; hence the recommendation to the novice not to meditate upon or yield to these three *chakras.* The buddhic man will, however, be their master, and will make use of their connections and vital powers.

Mumukshutwa.

The desire for liberation from the limitations of incarnate or manifested existence. This is not desire in the ordinary sense, which is desire for something, but is the inward awakening of spiritual perception whereby we become very conscious of the inadequacy of our present state of being, of consciousness and of happiness. It becomes so clear and strong that one is not able to picture anything now known, however idealized, as satisfying. It could be described as the awakening of spiritual hunger. This is the fourth of the Vedantic requirements for the correct and successful pursuit of realization of Brahman. (See under Sādhanā).

Muni.

One who practices silence *(mauna, q.v.),* or abstention from speech. The term is often used for a rāja-yogī or a philosopher, because he is thought of as being intent upon truths which are metaphysical beyond the range of comparison with ordinary facts of the body and mind. Such a person may speak or talk with reference to what can be talked about and still be called a *muni.*

N

Nādas, The Five or Seven.

Sound *(shabda)* has to be thought of as everywhere, just as in the springtime there is a simultaneous movement, and everything breaks into song. There is thus a song of peace in the cosmos, as well as the noises of war in all the little conflicts or movements of chaos. In the soul or mind of the yogī there is such a movement, and the noises of chaos are to be replaced in all respects, by the songs of cosmos. He must never forget that in the mere absence of the noises of chaos there is no attainment, and that only in the hearing of the song of cosmos is there attainment. This applies at all levels of body and mind, though the song (like touch and sight) is always within. It may be said indeed that man is never incarnate in the body, only in the mind, and the body is never a home for him but only a toolshed.

The yogī has to listen to his inner voice in several manners —some say five, some seven, some ten, which is a matter of classification. Some define them as the result of relatively outward or material practices; others relate them to *mantras,* others to inner meditations, going even as far as "the voice of the silence." In the last case, from a Buddhist work, we are told that the aspirant must hear the voice of his inner god in seven manners, which are, briefly, like a nightingale, a silver cymbal, the sound in a shell, a *vīnā*, a bamboo flute, a trumpet and thunder; the last of these, it is said, swallows up the others so that they are no longer heard. This could be symbolical of the sound in the silence growing stronger and stronger, surely a very mystical saying, especially as it adds that then the aspirant is merged in the One.

In another case—a minor Upanishad; a Hindu work—there is first a sound like "chini," then another like "chinichini," then a bell, then a conch, then a lute, then cymbals, then a flute, then a small drum, then a double-drum, and at last thunder. Another authority gives the order as like tinkling ornaments, kettledrums, bells, horns, flute and *vīnā*, and the yogī is told to give his attention to the subtler sounds. Another mentions the sound of the sea, clouds, water-falls, drums, bells, horns, flutes, *vīnās*, and bees.

Some teachers instruct their pupils to close the ears with the thumbs, the eyes with the index fingers, the nostrils with the middle fingers and the lips with the remaining four fingers. After a little practice, it is held, there will be a sound like the hum of a bee, then a flute, then a *vīnā*. With more practice there will be the sounds of bells, and afterwards thunder. The mind of the yogī becomes absorbed in these sounds, so that he does not notice other attractions.

The term *nāda* is also used to describe the prolongation of the sound when, for example, *Om* is recited.

Nādīs.

Channels in the subtle body. (See under *Sushumnā*).

Nāga.

One of the minor vital airs. *(q.v.).*

105

Nāmarupa.
(Literally, name and form).

This refers to the character of everything in the creation or manifestation. There is a difference between the two terms, inasmuch as form refers to the objective existence while name refers to the reflection of that in the subjective life or mind, where the name may stand as a symbol (a conventional, almost an algebraical, symbol) of the form and be used in the absence of the thing for mental process or manipulation concerning it.

The term is generally used with the thought in mind that what is referred to is in the field of *māyā (q.v.)*, and is not the real. The whole universe is considered to be transitory and nothing but the sum of the karmas of all the beings in it.

Neck Exercises.

As explained under Relaxation *(q.v.)*, the balance of the head *(q.v.)* depends very much upon the condition and habit of the muscles of the neck. For this purpose, the present writer has drawn up the following set of exercises:

(1) Sitting upright, slowly turn the head to right and left several times, pausing at each side to give just a little, very little, extra pressure. (2) Keeping the head straight up, not raising nor lowering the chin, push the chin and the whole face forward. Then, without leaning the head back at all, but keeping it vertical, bring the chin and face far back. Both movements are to be gentle, with a pause and a very little extra pressure. (3) Lean the head sideways, the left ear over the left-shoulder, so that a little pull and stretch is felt on the other side of the neck. Then slowly and gently move the head over, bringing the right ear over the right shoulder. (4) Lean the head forward, lowering the chin towards the chest. Then move it over until it is leaning back with the

mouth open. Again the gentleness, pause and slight pressure. (5) Lean the head forward, lowering the chin. Then slowly roll it round, first one way then the other. (6) A relaxing exercise for the neck. Lean the body forward, with the hands on the knees. Let the head loll forward by gravity, relaxing the neck. Then slowly rotate the body so that it leans to the right, to the rear, to the left and forward again, keeping the neck relaxed and letting the head roll by gravity. The jaw is also relaxed, so that the mouth falls open or shuts according to the position in the circuit. Repeat in the reverse direction.

These exercises may be followed by the relaxation of the face *(q.v.)*. They should be done for a few minutes every day, until they are no longer needed. Gentleness must be emphasized; one must take care never to *force* the neck at all, without the advice or help of a competent osteopath or chiropractor. These neck exercises, and some others, can be done with great benefit when on the toilet seat, for then use is made of otherwise wasted time, and also this tends against the impatience that is rather common, and harmful, in the performance of a most important eliminative function. Realizing the value of this, the wise will not mind its mention here.

Nidānas.

A series or concatenation of causes. Twelve, often referred to as the causes of misery, are listed especially in Buddhism, covering an entire cycle of material existence, namely, (1) ignorance *(avidyā)*, which is the awakening of the whole process, (2) the activation of the habit-molds *(sanskāras* or *sankhāras)*, in the three worlds —mental, emotional and physical—, (3) recognition of objects *(vijnāna* or *vinnāna)*, (4) the setting up of names and forms *(nāmarūpa)*, (5) the awakening of the six organs of sense *(shadāyatana)*, (6) contact with things *(sparsha* or *phassa)*, (7) feelings of pleasure or pain therefrom *(vedanā)*, (8) desire to enjoy or to avoid *(trishnā* or *tanhā)*, (9) attachment and activity *(upadāna)*, (10) coming to birth *(bhāva)*, (11) condition and class of the body *(jāti)*, and (12) the series of decay *(jarā)*, death *(marana)*, grief *(shoka)*, lamentation *(paridevana)*, pain *(duhkkha)*, and dejection or mental affliction *(durmanas)*. This is the condition of a lifetime, the recurrence of which will be prevented by the yoga which is union with knowledge or wisdom, or the destruction of ignorance, attainable by following the noble eightfold path *(q.v.)*. It is the abolition of this set of causes which is alluded to in the term *nirvāna (q.v.)*.

Nididhyāsana.

Profound meditation. This is the third of the three practices recommended in the Vedanta schools to the student who has performed the preparatory disciplines (see *sādhanā)*, the first two being reading or hearing *(shravana)* and thinking *(manana)*.

Nidrās.

Ideas obtained during sleep, which would be for the most part dreams, which have no basis in actuality.

Nirodha.

Control or government of ideas *(vrittis, q.v.)* in the *chitta (q.v.)*.

Nirvāna.

The Buddhist term for liberation, but the etymology of the word (nir-va, to blow out) indicates only negatively the attainment made in "reaching nirvāna," in order to avoid the ascription of anything in the "blown-out" region to the new state. The Buddha, on reaching this enlightenment, is reputed to have said: "I, Buddha, who wept with all my brothers' tears, laugh and am glad, for there is liberty." He also added the advice: "Sink not the string of thought into the fathomless: who asks doth err; who answers errs; say naught."

Still, the term does occur in Hindu scriptures, such as the *Bhagavad Gītā,* believed to have been spoken, though not written down, five thousand years ago. The Hindus do, however, permit the thought that this state is union with Brahman and his *sat, chit* and *ānanda (q.v.).*

Not-self, The. (Anātmā).

All that field of existence with which body and mind are concerned, including the very body and mind themselves, are the not-self. As such they are only means of education, or rather of self-education, toys to be discarded by the yogī at the proper time, when he is ready to deal with the self direct.

O

**Object—quality—action.
(Dravya—guna—karma).**

Everything is a compound of these three. It is not that an object *has* qualities and actions, for the qualities and actions *are* the object; indeed, the three are inseparable in fact, and should be so in our thought or opinion as to what is there, or here. Everything has action, according to its circumstances; thus iron acts on certain acids, though many persist in saying only that the acid acts on the iron. So action and reaction are fundamental in nature, and static objectiveness, though present, is not the basis of the other two. Everything acts according to its own nature; if a man throws a stone and breaks a lamp, who broke the lamp, the stone or the man? Both in combination, the stone by being a stone, and the man by being a man, each being free to be what it is. Yoga requires such realism in our thinking, and the non-adhesion to old fixed ideas.

**Observances (niyama),
The Five.**

These are cleanliness of body and mind, contentment, body-conditioning *(tapas),* study of self *(swādhyāya),* and attentiveness or purity of mind *(prasādana).*

When successful these five result in (1) health and self-protectiveness from the bad magnetism of others, high-mindedness, one-pointedness, mastery of the senses and fitness for vision of the Self *(ātmā)*, (2) the highest form of pleasure, (3) the decline of impurity and superior attainments of body and senses, (4) contact with the wise and good, the adepts and desired divinities, and (5) the power of contemplation *(samādhi)*.

Obstacles, the.

Patanjali lists the following as obstacles to successful contemplation: Disease, dullness, indecision, carelessness, sloth, worldliness, mistaken views, losing the way, and instability. They are all classed as due to splurging *(vikshepa)* of the mind *(chitta)*. They are accompanied by distress or pain, discouragement or despair, and disordered inbreathing and outbreathing. For the purpose of preventing them there should be the practice of one truth. This is usually taken to mean the constant memory of the real man as one and independent, or the following of a single main purpose in life, to which other things become polarized or for which they are directly or indirectly used, or again, the cultivation of clearness or purity of mind *(prasādana)*.

Occultism.

Knowledge pertaining to what is beyond the senses of the body, that is, the unseen *(adrishta)*, and the application thereof to practical living.

Occult Powers, The Eight.

These are a standard set of eight *siddhis*, accomplishments, perfections, or attainments— powers of the mind in relation to the world. Patanjali does not recommend the yogī to aim at these powers; on the contrary, interest in anything of the kind is regarded as defection from higher purposes which he should have in view, and positively injurious to *samādhi* (contemplation, *q.v.*). That the powers naturally arise when the yogī arrives at or near his goal is another matter, and the adept can then use them if he has occasion to do so. The list is:

To become at will very small *(animā)*, large, *(mahimā)*, light *(laghimā)*, or heavy *(garimā);* to be able to reach out for or obtain anything *(prāpti);* to have success with regard to any desire *(prākāmya);* to possess or control anything *(īshatwa)*, and mastery, or the power to direct affairs determined upon *(vashitwa)*. The last is most important, because all the things dealt with are in the region of personality, and in being master of all his affairs in this field the yogī or adept is sure of not being influenced from outside, but being entirely motivated from within. Such matters as smallness, bigness, etc. have reference to relativity, and the ability to see and deal

with the small and large, to approach the great fields of the minute or atomic and the large or astronomic, on their own level.

Although Patanjali has described the *siddhis* as accruing from *sanyama (q.v.)* and has given many instructions accordingly, he mentions that psychic powers (not necessarily these eight) can be produced also at birth, also by drugs, incantations *(mantras)*, or asceticism *(tapas)*. It is to be understood that *tapas* here mentioned is more extreme than the *tapas* which is a part of the yoga of daily life, the preliminary yoga, and a part of the five observances *(niyamas q.v.)*. Without the practice of the eight limbs of yoga, however, the effect of any psychic powers which might be obtained would operate only at low levels. For example, in the absence of the renunciation of desire to injure, lie, steal, be sensual or be greedy, required under the first of the limbs *(angas q.v.)* the psychic powers would only plunge a person into practices of black magic. As to severe austerities, these may thin down the material of the body, but this will not involve progress for the mind.

Occultism.

Knowledge pertaining to what is beyond the senses of the body, that is, to the unseen *(adrishta)*, and the application thereof to practical living.

Om.

The greatest *mantra (q.v.)* or word of power. When properly recited by a suitable person this word—which is the indicator of the divine power — produces great harmony in the body and in the mind. In the latter case the mental effects are greater when it is uttered only mentally, but in any case it should not be very loud, and it should be uttered in a floating way, as it were, not with force.

It is made up of three letters —A, U, and M. The two vowels *a* and *u* blend into *o*. M is sounded without parting the lips, so the whole word is sounded like "home" without the *h*, but somewhat prolonged according to the desire and intuition of the person reciting. The theory of *Om* is that as *a* is the first sound, made at the back of the mouth, and *m* is the last, made with the lips, and the *u* is of the nature of a glide between them, the word covers the whole range of vowel utterances, and since vowels are the power in speech and consonants represent only limitations or applications of the power this whole word is the expression of creation which indicates the presence of the Creator. Indeed, the whole range of creation is indicated, as the *a, u* and *m* are respectively associated with the divine powers or functions symbolized by the three devas or gods Brahmā, Vishnu and Shiva.

The aspirant is advised by Patanjali to repeat the word, not merely for the sake of repetition or the formation of a habit, but with thought upon its meaning. This meditation is given, says the teacher, for a two-fold purpose—that there may be the understanding of the nature of individual consciousness, and to procure an absence of obstacles to the attainment of the higher contemplation.

Om is recited by devout Hindus at the beginning of all prayers, hymns and words of worship or aspiration. It is also used at the end, or with the addition of *shānti (q.v.)* repeated three times.

Om Tat Sat.

This is a *mantra* mentioned in the *Bhagavad Gītā* as being used by "students of Brahman" at the commencement of various undertakings. The *Tat* (That), referring to the Brahman, reminds him of his high motive, and thus assists him in the rejection of what is unworthy of him. The *Sat* (reality or being) reminds him of the goodness everywhere, and so consecrates or sanctifies what he is doing, in this way bringing the undertaking within the field of *īshwara-pranidhāna (q.v.).*

Overself.

A term designed by Dr. Paul Brunton, to indicate that the holy fount of our being and root of our consciousness is still ourselves, is indeed our true self. The Sanskrit equivalent is *adhyātmā,* as in the *Bhagavad Gītā,* chapter vii, verse 29 and 30 and Chapter viii, verse 3.

P

Padmāsana. (The Lotus Seat).

Legs folded, with feet—soles upwards—on opposite thighs, hands on thighs, tongue against teeth, chin on breast or held up, gaze on tip of nose or straight in front (relaxed); or arms may be crossed behind the back with the hands holding the big toes.

Pain. (Duhkha).

In the *rāja-yoga* system pain is said to be caused by the conjunction of consciousness and what it sees. It is also pointed out that there is some pain in every such conjunction. The way out, however, is not by breaking the link, but through inward knowledge, strength and direction, gained through the practice of the eight limbs (*angas, q.v.*) of *yoga*. (See also under Pleasure). Much of our pain comes under the law of karma *(q.v.)*, in connection with which it is explained that harm due to us from wrong actions done in the past is cancelled out by good now being done.

Para, The.

That which is beyond. Used frequently by Shrī Krishna in the *Bhagavad Gītā* to indicate the state beyond the eightfold manifestation which has five kinds of matter and three functions of mind.

Paramahansa.

Highest or most perfect swan. A title bestowed by his followers upon a very great *guru* or teacher of yogic philosophy. (See *Hansa).*

Paramātmā.

The supreme *ātmā,* which, of course, is not different from *ātmā,* or *jīvātma, (q.v.).* The expression comes up because men so often use *ātmā* in the sense of the "lower self" and even the "higher self," both of which are not the real self, and therefore are the not-self.

Parināma.

Transformation in succession from moment to moment.

Patanjali.

Author of the *Yoga Sūtras* who lived about two centuries *B.C.*—not the originator but rather the codifier of the yoga philosophy and methods of practice, for many and various forms of these were very commonly known in very ancient times. Patanjali's system, ar-rangement, explanations and condensed expression have, however, proved so excellent and effective that almost every literate yogī is familiar with them, and looks to them for guidance. The *Sūtras* are in four Books or Chapters, dealing with contemplation *(samādhi),* the practice of yoga, the psychic powers, and independence *(kaivalya)* or liberation.

Path, The Noble Eightfold.

In Buddhism, the *dhamma (dharma)* or way of life which leads to release from suffering, which is to some extent always present as long as there is conditional existence.

The eight divisions are:

(1) Correct understanding, views, outlook, appraisal, judgment.

(2) Correct aims, motives, plans, considerations, decision.

(3) Correct use of speech.

(4) Correct behavior, conduct or actions.

(5) Correct mode of livelihood—the fulfilling of a defin-

ite role in life, which shall be unselfish, sensible, useful.

(6) Correct effort — some work of doing good.

(7) Correct intellectual activity—some study.

(8) Correct contemplation —the expectant poise of the mind which allows intuition and insight to begin.

Peace.

That state of mind in which there is no internal conflict and all outer things are received equally and equably. It is possible for the yogī to be at peace with the world in the midst of activity, and whether the world is at peace with him or not. (See also under *Shānti).*

Perception, Inference and Testimony.

These are the three ways described by Patanjali as the means of acquiring correct knowledge *(pramāna).* The last is sometimes interpreted as authority.

In spiritual realization only direct perception *(pratyaksha)* counts. The yogī first listens to the testimony of the scriptures *(shrūti),* then uses his judgment by thinking and inferring *(anumāna),* and finally reaches the point of direct first hand perception.

Philosophy, Systems of. (See under Darshanas).

Pingalā.

A channel on the right of the *sushumnā (q.v.).* This is described as coiling round the *sushumnā* and ending at the right nostril or at the *ājnā chakra.*

Pleasure and Pain. (Sukha-duhkha).

In the beginning a man is sluggish *(tāmasic)* and will not even stir himself to get food until the pain of hunger goads him to it. Then he discovers the pleasure of eating, and other pleasures, and he now becomes very energetic and even restless *(rājasic)* in the pursuit of pleasure, and so overdoes his pleasure. This brings on pain again, by which he becomes intelligent and learns to govern his actions and desires in orderliness *(sattwa),* in accordance with the moderation and harmony required by the laws of Nature.

Possessiveness.
(Abhinivesha)

The fifth of the five *kleshas,* or sources of trouble.

Powers obtained by Meditation.

Patanjali gives the following list of knowledge and powers arising from the use of mind-poise or *sanyama (q.v.):*

Knowledge of past and future. By *sanyama* on the transformation of things, which is triple, being of characters, qualities and conditions.

Understanding of the significance of sounds made by animals. By *sanyama* on the distinction between the sound or word, the object and the meaning.

Knowledge of former states

in life. By looking at the habit-tendencies or *sanskāras (q.v.).*

Knowledge of others' minds *(chitta, q.v.).* By looking at their mental images.

The internal state. By *sanyama* on the form of the body, the power of grasp on it being stopped, and light and the eye being disconnected. Many interpret this to mean that the body becomes invisible, but some hold that it has reference merely to leaving the body in trance and traveling in the subtle body.

The belief that a great yogī can become invisible at will, so as to preserve his privacy, is general in India, but as to whether it is done by manipulating the ether around the body or by casting an illusion on the observer involves a difference of opinion. From the point of view of yogīs it would be a matter of will power rather than manipulation, just as bodily functions such as walking are, with all of us, the body being obedient to the will, once the mental picture of walking has been made and the will has approved the picture and the action.

Knowledge of the time of death. By *sanyama* on the two kinds of karma *(q.v.)* —what has begun and what has not yet begun. Or by interpreting portents — something abnormal, or something outside the range of the senses.

Various kinds of strength. By *sanyama* on sympathy, friendliness, etc. These virtues are to be deliberately cultivated, and thus what they are in feeling becomes well known, and then meditated upon. The adage that virtue must be practiced for its own sake is unavoidable in this case.

The strength and other qualities of other creatures and things. By *sanyama* on the elephant, etc. An old proverb has it that what man thinks upon that he becomes. One could become a Master by meditating on the masterliness of the master, just as one is so much of a man as one realizes what it means to be a man. The contemplation of resting cats can relax us, of pebbles can smooth us, of posts can straighten us.

Knowledge of minutely small, concealed and distant things. By putting forth advanced sight, or looking for them in the inner light which arises when the eyes are closed. In this case there is only looking, not imagining nor demanding, which could distort the clairvoyance.

Nor should one expect vision, for the result may

come in words, or as symbols, or as what is apparently mere idea. A test of this is to take a dozen cards, shuffle them, separate one from the others and lay it face downwards; then look at the back of it, close the eyes and see what comes in the inner light. Record the result. Do this 120 times. If then you find more than 10 correct, and this on repeated tests, you are to some extent clairvoyant. The faculty grows rapidly with regular exercise. A warning is: during the test do not speculate or trouble about whether you are right or wrong or whether your faculty is growing or not; only at the end of the set test, say of 120 card layings, may one allow oneself to think of these matters.

In this light, which is, as it were, behind the eyes, there is vision of external things. By looking into the light at the top of the head, however, one may see the perfected beings beyond humanity and also obtain prescience or knowledge of the future, and answers to recondite questions.

Patanjali states that *sanyama* may be done on anything and produce, as well as clairvoyance, what we now call psychometry, that is, knowledge of other things connected with the object. Thus, for example, when a box containing a small article was purchased and sent by post to another town, and then put before a clairvoyant, he saw not only the object in the unopened box, but also the shop, the man who bought the article, and many other connected incidents. There may also be powers as well as vision, such as, for example, control of hunger and thirst by mind-poise on the pit of the throat.

Concerning oneself, *sanyama* in the heart center must be specially noticed. From this arises much knowledge about one's own character and tendencies, and develops much sensitiveness to the life around.

Most important, from the standpoint of the yogī who is intent upon achieving the goal of human life, is the *sanyama* upon oneself with a view to knowledge of the real man. The insight and visions respecting all objective things, though powers in the out-going mind, are obstacles to success in this highest contemplation.

Levitation is achieved by *sanyama* giving mastery over the vital air named *udāna* (*q.v.*).

Clairaudience is gained by *sanyama* on the connection between the ear and the ether (*ākāsha*). In practice there is an inner intentness, as hearing is the most spiritual and least external of the senses.

Astral travelling is gained by *sanyama* on the connection between the body and the ether (*ākāsha*, *q.v.*), or on something light and free, such as floating fragments of cotton.

The power of mind over matter arises from *sanyama* on the objective thing in five ways, referring to its objective character or form, its specific substance (such as of earth, water, etc.), its subtler nature as of materiality of operation, its relation to other things, and its effect or intention or usefulness. The first three of these are connected with the trinity of object, qualities and actions, the last two with its relation to other things, also the mastery of elements, perfections of body and non-obstruction of its function by earth etc.

Prabibhā.

Intuition or insight precedes the ultimate *viveka* (*q.v.*).

Praise and Blame.

It is recommended that one should receive praise and

blame equally and equably. It is not said that one should ignore them, as such, for they may contain some useful experience. An emotional rejection of them, except as such, would only be the replacement of one emotion by another of the same class.

Prajñā.

Wisdom, with spiritual understanding, the result of performing the eight limbs of yoga, leads on to the highest *viveka (q.v.).*

Prakāsha.

The inner light.

Prakriti. (Literally, the forth-made).

The material or manifest side of the universe.

The substratum of objective reality. The etymology of the word indicates the negative or non-actional, that is, substantive or material (in the widest sense), nature of everything—from *pra* (forth) and *kriti* (something made), but this does not mean the creation of forms, but of the principle of materiality, which is essentially inertia, which is, however, active in carrying the past into the present, and therefore in the present presenting a status quo (both static and dynamic) for the mind to act upon in its work of producing a different future.

Prakriti has three qualities (*gunas, q.v.*). These are *tamas* (static inertia, or matter), *rajas* (dynamic inertia, or force), and *sattwa* (formative possibility, or response to intelligence, hence form or combinative harmony, thus law in nature, its plastic ability to preserve forms). *Prakriti* as a principle, in the abstract, becomes *pradhāna*, the plastic fundamental materiality, when brought into relation with mind.

Prakritilaya.

A bodiless condition. (See under *Videha*.)

Pralaya.

The periodical sleeping-state of the universe, when all the "minds" or "lives" are resting, except those who have already reached liberation and have won their spurs, so to speak, in the divine region, beyond the dual manifestation of the matter-side (connected with *Brahmā: q.v.*) and the mind-side (connected with *Vishnu: q.v.*). The long alternating periods of world-rest and world-activity or manifestation are called the nights and days of *Brahmā*.

Pramānas.

Those ideas (*vrittis*) in the mind which are supported by perception, inference or testimony in such a way that one regards them as correct for all practical purposes. (See under Perception, Inference and Testimony.)

Prāna.

That *Vital Air (q.v.)* which is described as at the heart centre (see *Anāhata Chakra*), connected with the cardiac plexus, and therefore, it may be presumed, concerned with the health and strength of the heart and its work in the body. It is sometimes seen as of a yellow or coral color. This is not to be confused with breathing or respiration, for which the term *prāna* is also used (see under *Prānāyāma*).

Prānamayakosha.
(See under Kosha).

Prānāyāma.

Regulation of breathing. (See under Breath, Regulation of).

Prārabdha.

An adjective applied to that portion of a person's *karma* (*q.v.*) which has "ripened" and is already active in the field of his objective experience. This cannot be averted, but has to be dealt with in that field.

Pratyāhāra. (Withdrawal).

The holding back of the senses from the objects of sense. It is often observed that when the mind is engaged in reading or thinking, one may not notice quite loud noises, sights, odors, etc. This condition may be produced voluntarily by deliberate absence of curiosity, imposed as a mood of the mind in preparation for a period of practice of concentration and meditation. This withdrawal may be practiced by listening, for example, to the ticking of a clock, and then deliberately turning one's mental attention to some other subject. After a while one may happen to notice that one has not heard the clock in the meantime. One cannot watch one's senses stopping to influence one's mind, just as one cannot watch oneself going to sleep. After some practice, it becomes quite easy to turn one's attention away from unwanted surroundings—such as the noise and bustle of a train, dogs barking, boys shouting, or rivetting going on in a new building near by. When practicing concentration and meditation one first deliberately instructs both mind and senses to ignore outside interests, confident in the complete obedience of the senses.

Pratyaksha.

Direct perception—very necessary in yogic advancement, for one must not go too far in relying upon reason or inference. (See also under *Pramānas* and under Perception.)

Prayer.

The endeavor of one who feels weak to call upon or put himself in tune with a stronger power, and receive or draw help from it. Prayer has no place in the practice of yoga, which has no objective aims.

Pupil.

There are three kinds of pupils of the *guru* or teacher —highest *(uttama)*, middling *(madhyama)* and lowest *(atha-*

ma). The highest are those who know the teacher's intentions and carry them out; the middling are those who ask for and carry out his specific orders, and the lowest are those who do not even carry out the orders given. (See also under *Shishya* and *Guru.*)

Pūraka. (Literally, filling up). The inbreathing process in *prānāyāma (q.v.).*

Purusha. The real man, the enterer in the city of the body. This spirit is pure consciousness, also called, in Patanjali's teaching, the looker or looker-on *(drashtri, q.v.).* This conception of looker-on is apart from both subject and object, or rather what is commonly regarded as subjective is ultimately found to be a part of the objective world, though formless and immaterial. The erroneous notion that the mind is the seer reflects itself in the looker-on, which causes a conjunction of the seer and the sight, to destroy which is the object of the yoga practice.

Q

Qualities of Nature, the Three.

Tamas (stability), *rajas* (movement or restlessness), *sattwa* (order or harmony), which are called collectively the three *gunas (q.v.)*.

Quality versus Quantity.

In yoga it is quality that is aimed at, not quantity. One little thing done well is of more benefit to the inner man than a hundred not so well done, for in yoga we are not cultivating habits but powers. We find it useful to cultivate some good habits (*e.g.*, of breathing and posture, and good emotion and subjects of thought), but in practices of yoga the inner man should be at work improving his consciousness, and only incidentally changing or improving with thought, love and will, some part of this human mechanism, which is a collection of habits. One does not deny that human life is composed mostly of habits, which the consciousness enjoys without effort, merely following the instinctual actions, feelings and ideas rising from the past, but yoga is something more—it is the activity of the *inner man* and ultimately the transcendence of even that by union with or realization of what is beyond the mind. At all stages the lure and delusion of material greatness is to be avoided.

R

Rāga. (Desire).

This feeling or emotion of liking and desiring arises from the memory of pleasure connected with any idea or object.

Raga-Dwesha.

Personal liking and disliking of things and people, based generally upon previous pleasures and pains. These are to be given up by the yogī, as being based on ignorance, and leading to limiting attachment and desires. (See also under *Vairāgya*.)

Rajas. Force or energy. Dynamic inertia.

A quality or power in Nature, which causes things to continue their tendencies or habits of motion. It is seen in man as restlessness of body, excitability of the emotions and the flow of old ideas.

Rāja-yoga.

The system of yoga in which the man within asserts himself as the king (*rāja*) of all his mental and bodily possessions and powers. It aims at his realization of his status as master, and ultimately of his complete non-dependence on anything outside himself. This being so, the rāja-yoga philosophy does not allow that bodily practices can generate or improve mental powers or insights, though it agrees that they can lessen or remove certain obstacles and hindrances due to their own defects, or defects induced in them by wrong thinking and action in the past.

Reality, of the world.

Patanjali holds that things are real, because, although they are changing in form, there is a continuing substance. He argues that if an object were created by one mind and that mind ceased to cognize it, it would cease to exist. Further, minds are different kinds of being, as is shown when two minds regard the same object differently. Still further, an object is only known to the mind which is colored by it, and otherwise exists unknown. All the same the mind is not conscious, but is something seen by the consciousness, which is the real man *(purusha, q.v.).* Thus even the mind exists for the sake of something other than itself, but it does exist and

can function automatically by rearrangement of its contents. Formal logic shows some of its mind-mechanism.

Rechaka.
(Literally, emptying).

The outbreathing process in *prānāyāma (q.v.).*

Reincarnation.

The doctrine of rebirth, considered to be necessary to yoga, as only rarely—and as a result of efforts in previous bodies—can there be full union with the divine or Brahman. There must be a last time, of course, but that would be hard to judge, as in that last birth one may be getting over a last serious defect of character or, in other words, filling up a serious deficiency. In this there is some resemblance to a chicken pecking its way through its shell; all the pecks are of the same kind but it is the last one that breaks through.

Relaxation.

Though relaxation is not specifically mentioned as such in the old yoga books—probably because it is very natural for Hindus to be relaxed when not busy—there are nevertheless many indications of it, as, *e.g.*, in Patanjali's aphorisms iii 46 and 47: "Sitting is to be steady and pleasurable; by loosening of effort . . ." and in the corpse-posture *(shavāsana, q.v.).*

Yoga practice causes one to be considerably relaxed at all times with regard to the limbs or organs which are not in use at a given time; *e.g.*, one then walks with the legs only. There is what may be called "relaxation into normal action," which the present writer has called "balanced musculature." Successful balanced musculature often needs to be established by some exercises, such as the muscular habit of holding one's shoulders and neck correctly (see Neck Exercises, also *Uddīyāna),* or the "relaxation in action" of the eyes *(q.v.)* and face *(q.v.).*

Rishi.

An inspired seer. One of the sages of the past through whose agency the sacred scriptures and great sayings were provided for mankind.

S

Sabīja. (Literally, with seed).

Referring to those forms of meditation and contemplation which result in a new platform with respect to the subject which has been dwelt upon.

Sachchidānanda.

The nature of That *(Tat)* as distinguished from This *(idam)*, the latter referring to anything whatever in the field of manifestation, either objective or subjective.

The term is a compound of the words *sat, chit* and *ānanda (q.v.).*

Sacrifice. (Yajna).

In yoga this term does not refer to ceremonials or sacrificial victims. It indicates a principle of life, most fully explained in Chapter III of the *Bhagavad Gītā,* wherein it is taught that in the cycle of Nature all creatures nourish and maintain one another, and among the higher beings, including Vishnu himself, the proper way of life is to give voluntarily what one has and is for the welfare of the world *(loka-sangraha).* It is in connection with this idea that the carrying on of one's domestic, social and professional duties in the right spirit is considered to be a very important part of the religious life. Even the maintaining of an excellent personality is not to be for selfish satisfaction; even also the gaining of knowledge, the giving of which is described as "greater than any material sacrifice." This unselfishness does not tell against personal happiness in any respect, but increases the four kinds of happiness — bodily, emotional, mental and ethical—and paves the way for the fifth—the spiritual—which is the only one that is undiluted. When the spiritual comes it will remove the taints of pain from all the others, so in the end the way of "sacrifice" is also the way of happiness.

Sādhanas.

Practices which are means or methods. Especially the four means to qualify for success in the pursuit of the means to liberation and attainment of knowledge of Brahman. The four are *viveka, vairāgya, shat-sampatti* and *mumukshutwa*

(q.v.). The term is also applied in general to the practice of all methods leading to the acquisition of psychic powers *(siddhis)* and the furtherance of other religious attainments.

Sahasrāra Padma, The. (Thousand-Petalled Lotus).

A name for the center of consciousness which is situated at the top of the spinal column of the head in every human being. In Sanskrit, *sarhasrāra-padma*. Its petals have all the letters of the alphabet twenty times, and are of all colors. It pertains to the very *ātmā* (and *Paramātmā)* itself. It is the seat of the unmanifested Shiva, beyond the deities of the six *chakras,* so that when *kundalinī* visits here and then returns back to her home at the base of the spine, going through all the *chakras* on the way, she not only restores to them their powers which became latent when she went through them on her upward journey, but she gives to them a new quality altogether, derived from her union with Shiva.

Sālokya.

Residence with God *(q.v.)*.

Samādhāna.

Polarization of the mind and life to the high purpose proposed in the Vedantic doctrine —the opposite of scattering one's energies and wasting one's time with disconnected attractions and interests. One of the six attainments. (See under *shatsampatti)*.

Samādhi.
(Contemplation, q.v.).

The third and highest member of the three inner limbs *(antarangas)* of the *rāja-yoga*. The complete agreement or coordination of all the contents of the mind with regard to a given subject of contemplation, such that no more thought about it is possible, but the consciousness is at its best, in a great state of expectancy without anticipation, leading on to the receptivity of conscious experience not experienced before.

Samādhis, the two.

These are called *Samprajnāta* and *Asamprajnāta*. That is, with knowledge, in the sense that there is an object, or some subject-matter of the mental attention, in the first, but in the second nothing objective at all.

In the *samprajnāta* there is also a subdivision into two. 1) with inspection *(vitarka)* or examination. This occurs when a word has been spoken and there is a desire to know its meaning and what the object or matter referred to is. After considering the word and its meaning at last knowledge dawns suddenly upon the mind, and one exclaims: "Ah, now I know—so-and-so." It must be noted that when the process begins there is merely something brought up for enquiry (as when one takes, for example, a subject from a book, such as the *Bhagavad Gītā*, to meditate upon); this primary state is one of mental *tamas*—like a dark room, or an unlighted object. Then comes the process of enquiry, which is mental *rajas*. Then comes the understanding—and with it the ceasing of enquiry—which is mental *sattwa*. This last condition is called non-inspectional *(nirvitarka)*, and is a *samādhi* with seed *(nirbīja)*, which means that finally the *samādhi* ends where it began, but with some illumination of the mind with reference to the object or subject-matter on which the mind *(manas)* has been working, and some purification or correction of the same in the mind *(chitta)* which has been receiving the results, to be retained in its storage or system of habits *(chitta-sanskāras)*. 2) With investigation *(vichāra)*. This is concerned with a subt-

ler significance. Having decided what the object is, and the mind having become quiet, it may remain for a time in *samādhi* on that object. Or, then or at some other time afterwards, it may open up another sort of enquiry with regard to that object, namely, the investigational *(vichāra)*. This deals with what is called the subtle *(sūkshma)* nature of the object. The subtle does not mean a finer in the material sense, such as a number 60 sewing cotton as compared with a number 12, or as an electron compared with an atom of hydrogen, but refers to the subjective significance, such as what the subject is for the emotions, or for the intellect (its class, similarity and difference, etc.), or for the causality, and finally what it is for the character and will of the subjective man or full mind consisting of thinking, feeling and willing. But this process of enquiry has to stop at the indefinable *(alinga)*, simply because it is a process of reasoning about something which, however is still definable. Again there will be light when the investigation or reasoning ends, and one again suddenly says to onself, "Now I understand." The contemplation of this understanding is the non-inspectional *(nirvichāra) samādhi*, and it is the supreme light attainable to the mind in its dealing with the world. It is *tamasic* in the beginning, when it is concerned with ideas read or heard about; then in the process of reasoning it is *rajasic*, but the *nirvichāra* stage of the contemplation is the *sattwic*. Again, however, the *samādhi* is with seed *(sabīja)*, as it delivers the consciousness back to the object with which it began.

The second, or *asamprajnāta*, contemplation or *samādhi* is still a process of the mind, but it is now looking up, or opening itself upward, to what is beyond all objectivity, whether gross or subtle. It is now facing the indefinable, which is none other than the real man or *purusha.*

It will be noted that when the process of *nirvichāra samprajnāta samādhi* has been done at all it leaves its own habit-mold or tendency *(sanskāra)*, which has overcome to some extent the earlier habit-molds. Now, in the *asamprajnāta samādhi*, there is still another habit-mold set up—that of attentiveness to the indefinable—which overcomes all the earlier habit-molds and sets up a chief tendency towards this kind of *samādhi*, making it easier all the time. All this leads on to a new perception *(viveka)*, which leads to independence *(kaivalya)*, which is indicated in the mind not by knowledge but by unaccountable joy *(ānanda)*, which, however, is self-knowledge, the consciousness of consciousness itself.

Samāna.

That *Vital Air (q.v.)* which

is described as at the navel
center or solar plexus (see
Manipūraka Chakra), connected with the epigastric plexus,
and therefore concerned with
the processes of digestion. It is
sometimes seen as of a green
color or like clouded milk.

Samatwa.

Evenness of mind. "Samat-
wa is called yoga" says the
Bhagavad Gītā. It is related to
the teaching that the wise man
receives in the same spirit all
the varieties of experience
which karma may bring to
him. There is then an entire absence of any feeling of antag-
onism or discontent, and so
arises a state of mind in which
one can see the good or use of
everything and obtain the best
that everything has to give. In
addition to that there is, of
course, peace of mind, which
is conducive to yoga.

Sāmīpya.

Nearness to God *(q.v.).*

Sanchita.

An adjective applied to that
portion of a person's *karma*
(q.v.) which is in storage, as it
were, awaiting its opportunity
to manifest in the environment.
Such *karma,* it is held, can be
averted by contrary actions
performed in the present, which
will neutralize it. For example,
cruelty done in the past can be
neutralized by kindness done
in the present.

Sānkhya Philosophy, The.

One of the six well-known
systems of Sanskritic philosophy, which contains a classified description of the 25 con-
stituents, principles or truths
(tattwas) of our world of experience, by the correct knowledge of which a man may reach
liberation *(q.v.).* This philosophy is specially notable in
connection with Patanjali's
rāja-yoga, as that philosophy
on which its terminology is
largely based. The word *sānkhya* means enumeration and
classification, so the system is

regarded as scientific, and is so considered in the early part of *Shrī Krishna's* teaching in the *Bhagavad Gītā* where he explains the relations of body and soul and speaks of his description as "according to Sānkhya," only afterwards adding his own special teaching. Chapter II, verse 39, onwards.

The twenty-five divisions, or *tattwas (q.v.),* are first two, spirit *(purusha)* and matter *(prakriti),* the latter then being subdivided as follows: (3) intelligence, *(mahat* or *buddhi),* (4) individuality or egoity or entification *(ahankāra),* (5) mind as co-ordinator and logical interpreter of sense-experience, (6-10) the five sense-organs *(jnāna indriyas),* (11-15) the five action-organs *(karma indriyas),* (16-20) the five gross elements (ether, air, fire, water and earth), and (21-25) the five subtle senses. (See under *tanmātras).*

activities. The sannyasī is one who renounces the fruit of actions, or acts without desires, but it is carefully explained that he should act from another motive instead, namely, wisdom, so that his actions will all be within the sphere of *dāna* (free giving), *yajna* (sacrifice, which is action for the welfare of others), *tapas* (actions for keeping one's own body, speech and thoughts in good condition).

The way of renunciation, which is the life recommended as the highest in the *Bhagavad Gītā* and other religious books. It is the renunciation of all desire for any reward or recompense for the good that one may do. It is not the cessation of all activities in the world; on the contrary the acts of giving *(dana),* of sacrifice *(yajna, q.v.)* and of *tapas (q.v.)* are strictly enjoined.

Sannyāsa. (Renunciation).
Putting aside possessions and

Sansāra.
The course of human ex-

istence through incarnation after incarnation.

Sanskāra.
(Habit-mold, or mood, q.v.).

A *sanskāra* is a habit, or the influence of the past in the present producing so-called habit or automatism. It is regarded as the psychic center of a piece of inertia, which psychic conditions acts as a mold governing the body, or a mood governing the flow of ideas at any given time.

When the will so determines, there is a transformation of the lower mind *(chitta)* into a state of relaxation in which it drifts away and along (associational flow of ideas), or into a state of control or flow to a center (a chosen subject) which is concentration. Such a state is a habit for the time being or, in other words, the will has established a habit for the control *(nirodha)*. The man who has learnt what concentration feels like can establish the state or mood, of "recall" or "return,"

which will then remain in force without his attention to it (because it is a habit) for the intended period. So one can be in the mood of concentration, or in the mood of spreading or drifting. The common or usual mood allows the habit of the flow of association of ideas (also called drift or spreading), but in yoga there is the practice of concentration or recall, and so the establishment of a new *sanskāra*. The flow of thought is now towards the center. Then, as moment succeeds moment, the same object is repeated or revived. When the subsided and arisen images are similar in the successive moments there is a "one-pointed" condition of the mind. The habit-mold causes this to be a peaceful flow of concentration, which then continues without attention, as a foundation for meditation *(q.v.)* and contemplation *(q.v.)*, or complete *sanyama (q.v.)*.

All the objects in the world, also the sense organs in man,

have their habits, because of their *sankāras*.

Sanyama.

The poising of the mind on an idea or thing by means of a combination of concentration, meditation and contemplation *(q.v.)* taken in succession. (See also under Powers, and Senses, Control of).

Sanyama, Highest use of.

The full and final knowledge and mastery for man results from mind-poise *(sanyama)* on the otherness from each other of the pure mind and the real man *(purusha)*. This is such a fine distinction or discrimination that it is not a difference of class (as, *e.g.*, lion from cow), nor a distinction of a particular within a class (as, *e.g.*, red cow from black cow), nor a distinction of place (as, *e.g.*, cow in the shed from cow in the field), nor a distinction of time (as, *e.g.*, cow of yesterday and cow of today). It is the distinction between pure being and limited or relative being, in which neither comparison nor causality take part. This involves the highest intuition, called *tāraka (q.v.),* beyond the conception of subject and object. It is pure consciousness knowing pure consciousness directly *(aparoksha* and *sākshātkāra).* It is then seen that even pure mind is not self. This knowledge becomes possible through the highest discrimination *(viveka).*

Sanyoga.
(Literally, joining together).

The conjunction in thought of the seer with the object seen. (See under *Ahankāra).*

Sārūpya.

Similarity to God *(q.v.).*

Sarvāngāsana.
(Posture of All the Limbs).

This is done by standing on the shoulders with the legs vertical and kept still, the back being supported by the hands, while the elbows are firmly on the ground, taking the weight.

Sat.

The reality, the true, *Brahman* (q.v.) or God. (See also *Chit* and *Ananda*).

Sat-Chit-Ānanda.

The three characteristics predicated of the Reality or Brahman—being *(sat)*, knowing or consciousness *(chit)* and undiluted happiness, joy or bliss *(ānanda)*. These are not to be thought of as three qualities, for each one of them is the other two as well as itself, and the Reality is of only one essence, though the human mind, looking at it as through a veil, erroneously calls it three in one.

Sattwa. Orderliness.

A quality or power in Nature, which causes things to retain their mutual relations or reactions, once these are established. Natural law and order. The same word is also sometimes used for mind, be-

cause of its work in establishing order in nature, as e.g. in the making of a clock, in which the parts are in orderly relation, or in the development of human and animal bodies. It is seen in man in the quiet and orderly functioning of the breathing, circulation of blood, digestion etc.—routine matters well coordinated and helpful to one another. An advanced example is the process of heredity.

Satya. (Truthfulness).

The second of the abstinences *(q.v.)*. This virtue makes for simplicity of mind and ease of memory. He who deceives others will end up by deceiving himself. The worst of deception is that it induces mutual mistrust and spoils social relations. One hears people say: "I cannot believe the parson since he subscribes to false doctrines, 'because they will do good,' and I cannot believe my doctor because he thinks that if I know about my disease I shall worry about it and make it worse." The yogī decides not to add to this trouble, but to be truthful to himself and others. It is not a question of right or wrong knowledge, but of truthfulness.

Sāyujya.

Conjunction with God *(q.v.)*.

Scriptures, The.

Fundamentally, the Vedas, which are held to contain the revelation of essential truth or knowledge. As a practical guide to the understanding of these, there is the "Threefold Support" *(Prasthāna-traya)*, which consists of the *Brahma* or *Vedanta Sūtras*, the ten great *Upanishads*, and the *Bhagavad Gītā*.

Self. (Ātmā).

Has distinctly two meanings among yogīs. There is the real self, the *ātmā* or *purusha (q.v.)*, and the false self, which is formed by an erroneous con-fusion of the real man with his instruments, the body and the mind. It is easy to watch the growing self-personality of a child, and see how in the beginning it is highly conscious without thought of self as an entity or something in the world, and then how it gradually builds the personality by finding out what it can and cannot do, by hearing what others say of it, and even by looking in the mirror, until in the adult it is very definite, and includes appearance, profession and many habits of body, emotions, and ways of acting and thinking.

A good personality is useful in the world, but the yogī regards it as not himself, and after he has attained a clear understanding of the difference between this real self and his false self, he gradually becomes less interested in the latter, whereupon the *kleshas (q.v.)* which sustain it become weaker and fade away, while the yogī's meditations on the real self lead him away from such questions as "Who and what am I?" which he needed in the beginning, and thus open the door to intuition and insight concerning the real self. He is now coming near to the point at which Nature will have nothing more to teach him, he will therefore need no further incarnations, and—the essence of the matter—the power of consciousness will stand firm in its own nature, the real man having attained his independence, *(kaivalya, q. v.)*.

In addition to being and knowing and happiness *(sat-chit-ānanda, q.v.)* the Self is often also credited with being stainless *(nirmalatwa)* and eternal *(nitya)*. Some also add six negative characteristics: the Self (1) does not exist (in the sense of being in and of the world of manifestation, either subjectively or objectively), (2) does not get born, (3) does not grow, (4) is not subject to changes, (5) does not decay, and (6) does not die.

Self-realization. (Atmavidyā or Purushajnāna).

Experience of the not-self can never inform us about the self, because it exists "for the sake of another" *(parārtha)*, being something created and destroyed, like a toy, while the self exists for itself. That is why we never see the self of another, but only his body, possessions, and actions. Hence the yogī, wishing self-realization, or to know himself, must seek *beyond* the mind.

Self-reliance and Devotion.

These two methods are not incompatible in the yoga teaching and practice. On the contrary it is considered that man's only right *dharma* (duty to himself as well as the world) is to use his own faculties without strain or unbalance and that only so will they increase, but at the same time his life is helped at all its levels by association with the respective levels of Nature, and of course

141

at the highest and unseen levels, and even at the divine level, though he cannot call upon or use this. A general principle is that man can act and make only what is below the level of his present attainment, but he can become increasingly responsive to and unified with what is above, though the initiative of the working through and in him of that which is above must be left to it, otherwise the taint of the below would mar it, or even prevent that higher from working in or through his life.

Senses, Control of the.

Control and direction of the senses is improved by mind-poise *(sanyama)* on their function, character, individuality *(asmitā)*, connections *(anvaya)* and utility *(arthavattwa)*. These five characters of each of the five senses *(indriyas, q.v.)* are respectively concerned with (1) the nature of the senses as bringing information, (2) their general character of sense-ness, (3) their individual kind or type, such as hearing, or seeing, (4) their relations with certain kinds of experience and parts of Nature, such as light or sound, and (5) the part played by them in the education of men.

Further, from *sanyama (q.v.)* on the senses there arise also increased quickness of them, their action without the bodily organs of sense, and mastery over the substances with which they deal.

Separateness.
(Avachchheda).

This is the great heresy in Vedanta and its *jnāna-yoga.* As the statuettes yet unborn are seen by the sculptor in the one block of marble, all of the forms in the universe are gateways to infinite unity when fully seen and known in the *samādhi* of the yogī. The progress of pure science is in the revelation of unity, and all increase of understanding is the seeing of more of that, just as all increase of love is the feeling of more of that, and all increase of the will is the service of more of that.

Serpent in a Rope.

A simile often used to indicate the erroneous state of our vision of the world. A villager comes along in the dusk of evening and sees on the path before him a serpent, but on closer approach he discovers that it was only a piece of rope.

Shakti. (Literally, power or ability).

Primarily, the fundamental powers or forces found or seen in the manifested universe. These are presumed to originate in some way from the one basis and source of all being, the supreme and only Brahman *(q.v.)* or Absolute *(q.v.)*, which is the uncaused cause of all that is. These forces of the manifested universe are often pictured as goddesses, being concerned with the world, which is negative (or feminine) to the three differentiations of power called Shiva, Vishnu and Brahmā *(q.v.)*, residing above the manifested universe. The flow of feminine or manifest powers does not, however, stop at the three which deal with the over-all departments of creation, preservation and destruction, in the matter-side and the mind-side of the universe, and the play of life between them which being fulfilled brings their business to an end, the three being pictured as Saraswati, the helpmeet of Brahmā and patroness of all the Arts, Lakshmī, the helpmeet of Vishnu and goddess of prosperity and welfare, and Parvati, the helpmeet of Shiva, in some aspects of the work appearing as Kālī. These *shaktis* go on ramifying even down to the minor powers represented by the letters of the alphabet which are represented on the petals of the lotuses or *chakras (q.v.)* in the human being, in which also goddesses as well as gods symbolically reside.

Popularly, the shaktis or powers which may come about at various stages of yoga practice may be classified as follows:

Jnāuashakti, having to do with the perceptive faculties, such as clairvoyance, clairaudience, telepathy, psychometry, and even the reading of the pictures in tea-leaves, crystals, embers and clouds, and various omens, which are essentially ways of stopping one's thought because one is dealing with accidental forms, not rational sequences.

Kriyāshakti, having to do with concentrated thought-picturing without thought-activity, but with in the background a material intention to change something or to manifest something. It includes materialization, which however usually requires the help of ectoplasm, or magnetics or odylic forces, and also healing or injuring by thought-power.

Ichchhāshakti. Will-power, which is essentially self-control, leading to abnormal control of the body, astral travelling, etc.

Mantrashakti. The power of sound or rhythm, vocal expressions, music, etc. Used in rain-making and other stimulations of nature and in many religious ceremonies.

Shama.

Pacification of the mind, so that it does not restlessly throw up past impressions, but remains quiet until called upon to function. One of the six attainments. (See under *Shatsampatti).*

Shankarāchārya.

The great exponent of Vedanta, as teaching the universal religion based on knowing of, knowing about, and knowing, the One Reality or Being "without a second." As the knowing is an attainment dependent upon voluntary effort, Shankara preached also a system of *jnāna-yoga*, union through knowledge. The date of Shankarāchārya is in much dispute, many of the pandits (learned men) contending that he lived and founded his monasteries *(mathas)* several centuries *B.C.*, while others (including most modern scholars) place him several centuries *A.D.*

Various works of great philosophical and religious importance have come down to us under his name, the chief being his commentaries on the *Brahma-Sūtras* and the *Upanishads,* though there are in his name also many popular works containing the essential truths of the Vedanta and its yoga more simply stated, among the best known of which are the *Crest-Jewel of Discrimination (Viveka Chudāmani)* the *Hymn to Dakshināmūrti,* and the *Knowledge of Self (Ātma-Bodha).*

Shānti. (Peace).

This word is often repeated three times at the end of a discourse or reading, and is then usually preceded by *Om,* thus: *"Om, shāntih, Shāntih, Shāntih."* The *h* at the end is sounded with a *very slight* breathing of the previous vowel, that is, a very brief *hi,* which does not make an additional syllable.

Sharīra.

The body. Man is described as having three bodies *(sharīras* or *dehas)*—static or dense *(sthūla),* subtle or fine *(sūkshma),* and causal *(kārana).* Subdivisions of these are the five vessels or sheaths *(koshas, q.v.).* (See also under *Upādhi).*

Shatsampatti.

The six accomplishments in which an aspirant to liberation is directed to use his will and determination in self-discipline and self-training. They are:

(1) *Shama*. Control of mind, resulting in calmness.

(2) *Dama*. Control of body.

(3) *Uparati*. Cessation from eagerness to have certain things and persons around one and therefore a willing acceptance of what the world offers as material for living with.

(4) *Titikshā*. Patience; the cheerful endurance of trying conditions and the sequence of karma.

(5) *Shraddhā*. Fidelity and sincerity therefore confidence in oneself and others.

(6) *Samādhāna*. Steadiness or one-pointedness, with all one's forces gathered together and turned to the definite purpose in hand.

These, along with *viveka (q.v.) vairāgya (q.v.)* and *mumukshutwa (q.v.)* are the four means prescribed by Shrī Shankarāchārya by which the aspirant to knowledge of Brahman becomes qualified to find his way to success.

Shaucha. (Cleanliness).

The first of the five observances *(q.v.)*. It is understood to apply to the mind as well as the body.

**Shavāsana.
(Literally, corpse-posture).**

In this one lies down flat on the back with the arms along the sides and no pillow. This is intended usually for rest, and is considered to be very valuable after physical exertion. To get the best results one must completely relax every part of the body, giving attention to part after part until they become inert, and not forgetting the neck, face, eyes, forehead and even the scalp, also the emotions and the mind.

Shesha. (Literally, the remains or remainder).

In the mythology, the name of the serpent representing time. Time offers successive opportunities, or cyclic phases, and ensures that what is not possible to have or to be simultaneously is possible successively, such as to be man and woman. It is much concerned with the power of concentration, the first faculty of the mind (related to *ahamkāra, q.v.*), by which we give our full attention to one matter at a time.

Shīrshāsana.
(The Head Posture).

This is simply standing on the head. A cloth is folded to give a somewhat soft support. The fingers are locked together behind the head, and the elbows are on the ground. Proceed slowly, with or without help.

Shishya.

A pupil of a *guru (q.v.)*. Persons who are lewd, adulterous, sinful, slothful, irreligious or ignorant are unacceptable as pupils. Accepted are those who perceive the distinction between permanent and tem-

porary values and aims, who are not governed by old habits of emotion and thought, who are willing to practice self-control for the sake of orderliness of body and mind, and who have a desire to escape from the inadequacy of their present existence by gaining and applying more knowledge about the nature and composition and goal of man. No great talent is required.

Shiva.

The third of the great gods or manifestations of divine power in the world—the other two being Brahmā and Vishnu (q.v.). This is the power called the destroyer, which releases the human being from the form which it no longer needs, by giving to it that satisfaction of consciousness which is the fruit of experience. This function or form of deity is thus the one especially looked up to and worshipped by yogīs who are seeking liberation. The explanation is that in life we have forms or objects put before us (the work of Brahmā), also minds infused with the will to live with those forms, to understand and appreciate them (the work of Vishnu), and thirdly the power to benefit by the experience, gaining an inward strength, at which point we cease to need the form (the work of Shiva). With regard to each item we have a series of gains—first *perception* of a thing, then *enjoyment* of it as the mind gains knowledge and power, and thirdly *attainment* of something in ourselves, some awakening of the possibilities of our consciousness. Most people are satisfied with the enjoyment of things, but the yogī goes further and seeks *attainment.*

This power of deity is equated to the *First Logos,* the divine will in manifestation, while Vishnu is the divine love, cherishing the *jīvas,* and *Brahmā* is the divine thought providing the orderliness or "laws" of Nature, including the great law of karma *(q.v.).* Because of the sequence of these three powers we have birth, life and death in the world of forms, with respect to each experience. An object comes, is dealt with, and goes. With thought we make something, with love we use it and with the will we set it aside and proceed to something else. Deep in our hearts we welcome this process; it is our will as well as the divine will; the yogī observes and encourages this knowledge of man's unity with the divine in himself.

Shraddhā.

Faith or confidence. This is one of the six attainments *(q.v.)* in the Vedantic system of preparation for the reading or hearing, thinking and meditation which will lead to liberation. It is not blind faith but confidence in the Vedanta, due to its reasonableness and effectiveness. (See under *Shatsampatti).*

Shravana. (Hearing).

Listening to or reading about

the knowledge concerning the self and God which has been handed down in the Scriptures, by seers and *gurus*.

Shrūti.

The scriptures. Literally, what has been heard, therefore a revelation, either from a divine source, or by a rishi or seer who has his knowledge from such a source. The term contrasts with *smriti,* what has been remembered and is of human origin.

Siddhāsana.
(The Adept Seat).

Body straight; legs crossed, one foot having the heel close to the body at the front, the other just over its ankle; gaze between the eyebrows (forward, relaxed—not focused), or eyes closed; chin on breast or erect.

Siddhis. (See Occult Powers).

Sleeping State, The.
(See under Avasthās).

Smritis. (Memories).

This term is applied to a large number of old books which are regarded as containing memories or records. The term is also used for those ideas in the mind *(vrittis, q.v.)* which are reproduced from past experience or thought.

Snake in a Dream.

The lesson of the snake in a dream is that although the snake is unreal and only a dream-snake it can wake one up into the normal waking state, and similarly, although the objects of the world are *māyās (q.v.),* they can serve to wake us to the reality.

Soul, The.

Another term for mind, but meaning the whole mind, including the powers of will, love and thought. This is also the "inner man" or the "higher self," which persists from incarnation to incarnation. It contrasts with body, which is in the full sense a bundle of habits, actional, emotional and lower mental.

Sound, the Inner.

Whenever there is movement there is sound. In the mind— as there is an effect in the astral light, even if no action of the body has been done—an action (thought) is always accompanied by its music, or perhaps we should say singing, as well as light and color. Even behind this subtle *(sūkshma)* effect there is the sound itself, for as in the gross or physical *(sthūla)* world, so in the subtle *(sūkshma),* the objective sound is no sound, but only a manifestation, which the mind has to translate into its own sort of objectivity or separateness, which is sound. Sound is the first veil, and therefore it is related to the deepest knowing, touch being the second, and sight the third. Being related to the first kind of divided or separated motion, hearing is (even in the physical body) the sense that is felt most intimate or inside. In the effort to hear finer and finer sounds (see *Nādas,* the five) the yogī finds himself going into this depth, as it were, which at the same time involves the inhibition *(pratyāhāra, q.v.),* though not intentionally, of both touch and sight. Mere absence of touch and sight does not, however, bring forth the sound in the consciousness. (See also *Nāda).*

It is because these senses belong to the mind, not to the bady, that they are thought of as goddesses or powers *(shaktis).* The term is appropriate, as it is the feminine partner in the formation of a home who conserves, guards and arranges the contents, and is in general the creative or harmonizing power in that field, which left to the male partner alone would generally be no home to live in but only a place to keep his tools and weapons, or, if a literary man, his books and papers.

Spine, The (See Merudanda, also Chakras).

Stages of Life, The Four.

(1) Childhood and learning, in which the faculties of the body, perception, etc. are principally being developed; (2) the "house-holder" period of busy family life, in which the development of the emotions predominates; (3) the preparation for retirement in which the intellect generally gets more cultivation by a period of thoughtfulness, and (4) the fourth stage in which these three are harmonized and the requirements of the inner man receive proper attention. Thus the life of the higher self or for the higher self is considered normally to begin in this fourth period—in the West at the approximate age of sixty-three. But the yogī combines all three at a much earlier age, and in some cases, when he comes from a previous life in which he has voluntarily devoted himself to yoga, may begin to do so even in childhood.

Spirituality.
(See under Divinity).

Sthūla. (See under Upadhis).

Subject and Object.

These represent the two sides of creation, the latter being the matter-side and the former the mind-side or life-side of Nature. These are both considered to be emanations from the one divine and ultimate reality, the uncaused cause of all things and beings; therefore both are powers, which can be expressed in modern terms as the power which brings the past into the present (which we believe to be the only sound definition of matter), and the power which brings the future into the present (which is easily seen to be the function of the positive mind). They correspond to the functions of Brahmā and Vishnu—object and subject respectively. The other member of the divine Trinity is pictured as Shiva, beyond both subject and object, so the yogī must open his mind as far as possible to this third alternative.

Success and Failure.

It is recommended that one should receive success and failure equally and equably, without elation or depression. After all, these are only extreme cases of what is happening every moment, and one must always be on guard when something unusual or extreme occurs. The yogī learns also that these two are equal from the standpoint of both the horizontal evolution of body and mind culture, and the vertical evolution of our consciousness. As much can be and in fact is gained from our own and others' failures as from the successes. From a lost game we also learn, the only advantage of success being that it stimulates and encourages. The yogī however, is self-stimulated, so failure does not depress him,

or cause him to miss the value of his lesson. It is, of course, the action or work that we are doing which is important. Even in college or school the student who is interested in his subject of study will achieve the required knowledge, and it is a disadvantage and disturbance for him to think about success or failure. As Shrī Krishna said to Arjuna: "Your business is with the work; not with success or failure."

Sufi Yoga.

A form of aspirational practice among the mystical Muslims, having the aim of losing oneself in God, by love of God. First there are seven "stations" to be passed through by overcoming, to be done by the mystic's own endeavors; then there are ten "states" to be received from God, these not being in the power of human nature to produce for itself. The simplest list of stations is meditation, nearness to God, love, fear, hope, longing, intimacy, tranquillity, contemplation and certainty. Very much use is made of music among the Sufi mystics especially as their undertaking is one of love, not of reason.

The ten "states" are—meditation, nearness to God, love, fear, hope, longing, intimacy, tranquillity, contemplation and certainty.

In the end the constant thought or remembrance *(dhikr)* of God, will lead to union *(tauhid)* with Him, in which there will be the passing away *(fana)* of all human qualities or nature, and then the only continuance will be that of God Himself. It is easy to see in this a similarity to Buddha's doctrine of nirvāna, and that of liberation of the Hindu schools.

Sukha-Duhkha.
(Pleasure and pain) (q.v.).

Sukhāsana. (Literally, pleasant posture).

This is convenient for those who wish to sit on a carpet but find that their limbs are too stiff for comfort in the cross-legged form of sitting which is common in the Orient. In this posture one uses a long scarf or strip of cloth, which is passed round the small of the back and tied round the knees in some form to support their weight. It thus permits the knees to be considerably raised up. The hands then rest with palms together on the cloth in the valley between the knees.

Sūkshma. (Subtle or Fine). (See under Upādhis).

Sushumnā.

A channel *(nādī)* in the subtle body which goes straight up the interior of the spine, starting from the basal *chakra* *(mūlādhāra)* *(q.v.)*, up to the interior of the head. Inside it is a finer channel, named *vajrinī-nādi*, and inside that another named *chitrinī*. The last is spoken of as being as thin as a thousandth of a hair, but on it are the *chakras (q.v.)* and up it *kundalinī (q.v.)* proceeds. The opening at the base, blocked by *kundalinī,* is called *brahma-dwāra* (door of Brahma).

Outside the *sushumnā* are two other channels, *pingalā* on the right and *idā* on the left, coiling upward and uniting at the *ājnā-chakra.*

The three are sometimes considered to be symbolized by the caduceus of Mercury, but that symbol may also be used for other trinities.

Sushupti.

The deep sleeping state. (See under Avasthās).

Swādhishthāna Chakra, The.

The wheel or lotus at the level of the genitals. It has six petals of orange-red color, bearing the letters b, bh, m, y, r and l. In the colorless center there may be a picture of a *makara* (a large aquatic animal resembling a crocodile and a whale or a dolphin, which in general literature is also regarded as an expression of the god of love), which in-dicates a fluidic or watery power or strength. The *bīja-mantra* is *vam.* The deities to be venerated and served with devotion in this case will be connected with Vishnu and therefore with the power of wisdom and love, but in the early stages subject to outward temptations and thus very liable to the lower form of love, called *kāma* (desire), as explained under *Mūlādhāra (q.v.).*

Swādhyāya.

Self-study, from swa, one's own, and ādhyāya, study. Commonly thought of as study of one's own scriptures, but in the larger sense it covers all study concerning the true nature of man.

Swapna.

The dream state. (See under Avasthās).

Swastikāsana.
(The Swastika Seat).

Legs crossed; feet between the calves and the thighs; body straight.

T

Tamas. (Stability).

Static inertia. A quality or power in Nature, which causes things to remain the same from moment to moment. It is seen in man in the form of sluggishness or laziness of body, emotional apathy and mental prejudice.

Considered as one of the three qualities *(gunas q.v.)* of the material world, it is the *static* inertia which is seen in the carrying over of material forms from the past into the present. In its work of bringing changes into the field of living, which is the present, the mind makes use of the static inertia, as the basis of its new forms, as well as of the dynamic inertia or routine force *(rajas)* in creating more and more integrated or harmonious forms *(sattwa)*.

The term *tamas* is applied to anything which shows a preponderance of static inertia, as, for example, a *tamasic* person is one who is lazy or sluggish. (See under Pleasure and Pain).

Tanmātras, The Five.
(Literally, mete-ings of That).

Five fundamental principles or subdivisions or types on the matter side of things, corresponding to the five sensations

155

(of hearing, touch, sight, taste, and odor) which appear in consciousness, and so giving rise finally to the five sense-organs (ear, etc.) and the five corresponding states of matter (ether, air, fire, water and earth).

Tantras.

Certain treatises on yoga offering methods closely related to those of the *Laya-yoga* (*q.v.*). The system contains many formulas for the worship of deities—which are, however, symbolical—with a view to the use of powers, and is therefore somewhat mechanically magical, as the name implies, *Tantra* being a loom or the long threads on it, and thus a prescribed course, routine or mechanism.

Tapas.

One of the regular observances (*q.v.*) to be carried out by the would-be yogī in daily life in the world. The word comes from a root which means to heat or make hot, and thus it means to be ardent or full of effort. It is sometimes called purificatory action, because it burns up impurities. In the *rāja-yoga* system it has reference especially to the body, and so it is body-conditioning. It is often translated "austerity," and is so taken and misapplied by many inferior would-be yogīs in India, who then carry the idea to excess, even to the point of inflicting injuries upon their bodies. For luxury-loving people the proper care of the body, to keep it in thoroughly good condition so that it will not disturb the meditations that *rāja-yoga* requires, may look very much like austerity, but that the idea of austerity as such is remote from the teaching of Patanjali is seen from his description of the excellencies of the body, which include correct form, beauty and strength.

Tāraka. (Literally, a star).

Refers in *rāja-yoga* to the light between and in front of the eyebrows which is seen in meditation. The pupil of the eye is also called *"tāraka."*

"Tat twam asi."

The famous saying "That thou art." The aspirant should first meditate on *That,* which is Brahman or *Paramātmā* as distinguished from *This,* which is all the manifestation. Then he can be told, "That, thou art." If the teacher had said to him merely "Thou art That" he might have started off with the thought of the thou which he commonly thinks himself to be and have ended up with a wrong notion, but as it is he is taught, "That is what you really are, though you may have at present the erroneous notion that you are this you." When the aspirant is able to say *"So'ham"* (sah=That; aham=I; am being understood)

he has attained what the teacher desired. Another response having the same meaning is "Aham Brahmāsmi" (aham=I; Brahma; asmi=am).

Tattwas.
(Literally, That-ness).

True state or condition of anything. When applied to matter it means the five ultimate impulses in which originated the five states of matter (ether, air, fire, water and earth) which correspond materially to the basic impulses of the sensations of hearing, touch, sight, taste and smell. All five of the *tattwas* correspond to and form the *lokas* for the inner or invisible principles of man.

When applied to the self (*ātmā*) it refers to its real nature as being one with the supreme self (*paramātmā*). In this sense we also have such compound words as *tattwadarshin* meaning one who sees this truth. (See also under *Sānkhya*)

Telepathy.

The direct communication of emotional states and thoughts from one person to another. This takes place normally, for we live in a sea of other people's emanations in this respect, but the thoughts are usually not very coherent and not long-lived. Their influence is largely dependent on the principle of like attracting like. Strong minds having clear thoughts produce the most definite and sustained effects in this region, and this accounts to some extent for the fact that two or more people sometimes come forth with the same new ideas about the same time, as groups of thinkers are mutually stimulated and assisted at certain times. When there are masses of people, as in crowds sometimes, one may be much swayed by a feeling or idea (generally not good) which can then develop to dangerous proportions with very imperfect rationality. Confusions and agitations of feeling and thought are also infectious and contagious in this way.

In experiments and the practice of telepathy familiar images are best in the beginning. When two people plan an experiment together, fixing a daily time and alternating their receiving and sending, they will do best not to compare notes until the end of two or three months. In all these experiments — in which the success should increase with exercise and time—much depends on one's being very unselfconscious.

Temperateness.

"Yoga," says the *Bhagavad Gītā,* "is not for the excessive eater, nor for one who avoids food too intently, and not for one addicted to excessive sleep nor wakefulness. Yoga becomes the destroyer of pain for one whose food and recreations are appropriate, whose efforts in actions are appropriate, whose sleeping and waking are appropriate."

Thinking.

This is greatly important in yoga practices. In the *rāja-yoga* meditation is complete thinking on some topic or object (see under *Dhyāna*), while in the *jnāna-yoga* of the Vedantists much thinking is the first inward or advanced step towards the knowing of Brahman. (See under *Vichāra*).

Titikshā.

The endurance or acceptance of the present conditions of one's karma with entire non-antagonism, so that there is no discontent or impatience. One of the six attainments. (See under *Shatsampatti*).

Treasure, Hidden.

The lesson of the simile of hidden treasure is that this will not come out of the ground by simply calling it. We must have reliable information as to where it is, then remove the stones and dig.

Tree, The Ashvattha.

The famous bo-tree at Buddha-gayā in India, under which Gautama Buddha gained his enlightenment.

The *Bhagavad Gītā* and other scriptures refer to a symbolical ashvattha tree, which stands for the entire manifested creation, having its roots in the "heavens" above and its many branches and branchlets extended downwards into the world of men and Nature. The yogī has to cut off this tree of manifestation at the very root with the axe of non-attachment, which arises from the knowledge of the nature of *ātmā* and Brahman.

Trouble, The Five Sources of.
(See under Kleshas).

Turīya, the fourth state.

Reached in meditation when the consciousness goes beyond the workings of *manas* (thought), *buddhi* (insight or wisdom concerning the subjective), and *ahankāra* (interest in separateness). A state which cannot be described in terms of idea, love or the will. The three states of consciousness preceding this successively can be described as thinking involving variety, loving involving duality, and willing involving unity. (See under *avasthās*).

In popular thought, *turīya* is a fourth state beyond the three commonly experienced as waking, dreaming and deep sleeping, in the first of which the objects of the world are encountered, in the second only those in the mind itself, and in the third not even those in the mind.

Tyāga.

Giving up possessions and activities. A *tyāgī* is one who renounces the world, but for the full meaning of this see under *Sannyāsa*.

U

Udāna.

That *Vital Air (q.v.)* which is described as at the throat centre (see *Vishuddhi Chakra),* connected with the pharyngeal plexus, and presumably concerned with the muscles of the chest which operate the bellows for respiration, or lungs. The color sometimes seen here is a pale or whitish blue.

Uddīyāna.

Training of the abdominal muscles. (See under *Mudrās).*

Ugrāsana.
(The Powerful Posture).

Legs stretched out, a little apart; head held in interlocked hands with the forehead placed down on the knees, or the hands may hold the toes.

Unity.

Unity means something more than a collection of things made into a unity, such as, let us say, a sack of coal, or a clock, or a stamp collection. Unity is a power of interior binding, such as is seen in a human body or animal body. Unity is one of the three divine powers, the other two being harmony *(q.v.)* and variety *(q.v.).* The aim of yoga is realization or direct experience of this Unity.

Unmani.

A state of trance, or abstraction from the body; the result of *kechari mudrā (q.v.)* and other such practices. Called sometimes "the yoga sleep."

Upādāna, The.

The unchanging substance or material of which all things are made (as a pot is made of clay or a bracelet of gold), which is nothing but the very Brahman himself.

Upādhis.

In philosophy it means a distinguishing characteristic. With reference to man it thus becomes that which marks his presence in the various departments of living, his whole body in the sense of his expression, by which he is seen and known. Man has three of these bodies or states of being: the causal *(kārana upādhi)*, the subtle *(sūkshma upādhi)* and the gross or dense *(sthūla upādhi)*. These three are sometimes called the three *sharīras* or *dehas (q.v.)* as the words *deha, sharīra* and *upādhi* are synonymous.

If we consider the four kinds of distinctive departments in which man's expression appears, we have his *sanjnā*, (state of mind in the deepest sense), his *gunas* (qualities), his *kriyas* (actions), and his *jāti* (status among many varied conditions of life in the world). The last arises from his *karma (q.v.);* the *kriyās* are his current actions done by the dense body *(sthūla);* the *gunas* are the qualities shown in his subtle body *(sūkshma),* and the *sanjnā* is his essential state of being or what could be called in modern terms his evolutionary status, or in older terms his degree of awakening, or fulfillment.

Upanishads.

Certain books attached to and forming a portion of the

Vedas, which deal especially with the more mystical teachings, the nature of Brahman and the relation of man to Brahman.

Uparati.

The cessation of personal desires. One of the six attainments. (See under *Shatsampatti*).

V

Vairāgya.

Variously translated as uncoloredness, dispassion, desirelessness, detachment, indifference, etc. It has reference especially to the emotions. The mind should not be colored by its circumstances or habits. Uncoloredness should be practiced, so that there may be clear unbiassed thinking or meditation. The higher uncoloredness is that which occurs when thinking is not affected by desires for something stable, something exciting, or even something orderly, on account of knowledge of the real man or self *(purusha)*. It is connected with the word *rāga*, which means a liking for things, in contrast to *dwesha*, a disliking or hatred—*rāga* meaning dye.

Vāk or vāch.

Speech; an utterance or saying. *Vākya* means a sentence, and *Mahāvākya* a great saying, especially a great saying from the Vedas having reference to *Brahman* (q.v.), such as *"Ekam sad vipra bahudhā vadanti,"* (There is one Reality; the sages speak of it in many ways).

Variety.

One of the three divine powers, the other two being unity *(q.v.)* and harmony *(q.v.)*. In

the scriptures it is stated that
the One willed to be many, and
then variety came into being.
There could not, however, be
variety without individuality,
which implies unity. In the
creation stories, the sustaining
of variety is entrusted to Brash-
mā, the sustaining of harmony
is entrusted to Vishnu, while
the unity seen in the total
(whence none can escape) and
in the individual is the silent
presence of Shiva.

Vāsanās.

Commonly regarded as de-
sires, but really habits or tendencies of desire *(q.v.)*. These
are to be overcome as much
as possible, and *dharma (q.v.)*
is to take their place. When
the high powers of the human
soul (thought and love) are
not indicating the desirability
of some thing or action, the
desire nature should remain
quiet, just as the body remains
quiet until the inner man au-
thorizes an action.

Vedānta.

The end of the Vedas, end
(anta) meaning the highest and
final point of the teaching
given in the Vedas. A system
of philosophy based upon those
teachings, in which *jnāna-yoga*
(yoga by knowledge) predominates.

Vedas, The.

The original source-books of
the religion of India. Extracts
from the more mystical parts
of these—especially from those
portions of them called Upanishads *(q.v.)* are the basis of
the Vedāntic *jnāna-yoga,* as
well as the source of inspira-
tion for *bhakti-yoga.*

Vichāra.

Thinking—very serious and
long continued thinking. This
is positively prescribed in the
Vedānta schools, especially of
Shankarāchārya, to follow upon the course of self-training
or *Sādhana (q.v.)*. Without
thinking, it is said, there will

not be knowledge. Yet thinking is not knowledge; thinking stops when knowledge arises.

Videha and Prakritilaya.

It is possible to retire from the undertaking of yogic contemplation at any state on the journey, or rather pilgrimage, with the enyoyment of the state of consciousness so far attained, and remain bodiless or without incarnation for a long time. In such case there is the enjoyment of the state of consciousness of mind, already attained but no new experience. This is considered to occur to some extent between incarnations for all thoughtful and good persons, in which case the contents of the mind are provided by all that is interesting to the higher mind, heart and will, and these are material for reflection and meditation, which is then without effort. These memories include all incidents from the recent lifetime in which operations of goodness, truth and beauty have played a part. This is a sort of heaven, and is beneficial in inward ripening of the mind. Even very old persons while still alive enjoy this state to some extent, when they become somewhat inattentive to what is going on round them, and very attentive to some of their quite distant memories, with regard to which the writer's own father when up in the nineties used to say that he got more out of the memories than he did out of the original experiences, as everything now meant so much more to him than it did before.

The case of the advanced yogī who wishes to rest for a long time is an extreme example of this. He becomes *videha,* it is believed, for thousands of years. Such persons still have the thought of themselves as the personal self so that pictures and enjoyments in connection with it occupy the whole scene of consciousness.

The term videha is also applied sometimes to the gods or

devas, who are liberated be- ings who have been men in the past. These beings are not sep- arate from the divine life, or Brahman, of which they are thought to represent various functions.

Another class of discarnate beings are described as ab- sorbed in Nature (*prakritilaya*). These also are considered to be in a state of suspension, but differ from the videhas in that they are interested in the con- ditions or elements of natural substances, such as air, water, or fire, not in the activities of the mind-side of nature. Such may be the case of persons of considerable power of medita- tion and contemplation, who desire the stable condition of earth, the fluid condition of water, the expansive condition of air, the radiant or vigorous condition of fire, etc. Their ideas are intent upon these ob- jective perfections, and their pleasure and desire are consid- ered to immerse them in these enjoyments for a very long time. Students are usually ex- horted to avoid these two states, and proceed by faith (*q.v.*) etc.

Videhamukti. (Liberation while disembodied).

While it is possible to be liberated and bodiless, it is not possible to obtain liberation while bodiless. The embodied condition is that in which the high point and power of free consciousness is reached in the act of concentration, carried through meditation into con- templation, and thence through the gate of *viveka* (discrimina- tion) into its full power and freedom from the need for any further concentrations or em- bodiments. There is a soupçon of this liberty at all stages of life, but people do not notice it. To notice it is great wisdom.

Vijnānamayakosha. (See under Kosha).

Vikalpa.

Imagination (*q.v.*). One of the five kinds of ideas, (*vrittis*) in the lower mind (*chitta*). The importance of this classification is that we have the ability to recognize imagination for what it is—a reproduction in the field of mental vision of things seen before, or a combination of such things. Thus we can speak of an imaginary thing as in the mind. Examples of the exercise and enjoyment of this faculty are seen in many literary productions, such as Shakespeare's *Midsummer Night's Dream,* Lewis Carroll's *Alice in Wonderland,* or the stories in the *Panchatantra,* the *Hitopadesha,* or *Aesop's Fables,* and of course, innumerable modern novels and stories.

Vikshepa. (See under Māyā).

Viparyayas.

Those ideas which on rising in the mind are immediately classed as wrong knowledge, as *e.g.* if someone were to say that the moon is made of green cheese.

Vīrāsana.
(The Vigorous Seat).

Legs crossed; left foot under the right thigh and right foot over the left thigh, or *vice versa.*

Vishnu.

The Puranic stories relate that after Brahmā had created the world he found it dead and motionless, so he prayed for help, and Vishnu entered into it (*vish* means "to enter") and filled it with life. This life was the great host of beings of the mind-side who were somewhere on the path of progress towards their perfection. Mind brought in time, and then there was change or motion. Vishnu is thus the principle of ideation, and is the divine spirit of the *jīvas,* beyond their minds. This is what may be called the second power or Logos in the world, but it was of course the first power which emanated and empowered this Vishnu, just as it emanated the third power or Logos named Brahmā. These divine powers may also be found under the head *Adhi* (*q.v.*).

Vishuddhi Chakra, The.

The wheel or lotus at the throat level. It has 16 petals of a lilac color (some say the color of fire seen through smoke), bearing the letters of all the sixteen vowels. The animal shown in the picture or design is a white elephant, which symbolizes or indicates the poised strength of the element named ether (*ākāsha, q.v.*). It is the region of ether, of circular shape and a whitish-grey color. The bīja mantra is *ham.*

In this *chakra* the deities for devotion will be connected with Shiva, this *chakra* being especially the seat of the will and the power of the inner man, yet, of course, having that background of Vishnu, the buddhic love and wisdom which is the basis and fundamental note of the inner man.

(See also under *Chakra.*) Here Shiva has the form of giver of happiness, of pure crystal color, with five faces, ten heads, three eyes, with many weapons and ornaments, one half of the figure having a female form representing Parvatī, also called Umā. It is to be remembered, however, that it is the Shiva aspect of Vishnu which is now being thought of.

Vital Airs. (Vāyus).

These are forces of Nature which vitalize the several departments of automatism in the human body, through the *chakras* and their related plexuses. The books list ten of these vital airs, but five of them are considered so important that quite usually one finds only "The five vital airs" mentioned. These five are named *prāna, apāna, samāna, udāna* and *vyāna,* concerned respectively with the centers and areas of the heart, the anus, the navel, the throat and the genitals. (See under the

169

several names for particulars of each of them.)

The general principle rests upon the fact that the bodily constitution of man is a trinity —the dense body, the etheric "double," as it is often called, and the vital force which connects them, the last two of which are called the *prānamayakosha* (see *Kosha*) in the Vedantic philosophy. The etheric double may be called "the brain of the body" because it contains the *sanskāras* (habits) which govern the unconscious functions of the dense body which are in the department of the sympathetic nervous system, so that it acts as a sub-conscious mind for that department, including what may be called the material memory. Thus the trinity carries on all the routine business of the body, such as respiration, digestion, circulation, perspiration etc. and the very important business of directing incoming materials into their proper places in the body,

so that in the replacement of old material the forms and functions of the body may be carried on or continued.

The vital airs flow strongly when there is harmony between the various organs and the conditions in the etheric double. This desirable state of affairs is spoiled from the outside when the body is subjected to unhealthy conditions (*e.g.* polluted air, indigestible food, or bad posture), and is spoiled from the inside by unhealthy thoughts and desires which taint the double, disturb its habits, and may even go so far in this as to cause psychosomatic diseases. This becomes possible because the *prānamayakosha* (*q.v.*) is very responsive to the *kāmas* (desires) in the *manomayakosha* (*q.v.*). The *prānas* or *vāyus* are thus a sustaining "life-force" in nature, and their vigorous flow when the human being treats both his body and his etheric double (*q.v.*) properly is one instance of "God helps those who help themselves."

The five minor *vāyus* are *nāga* (for vomiting), *kūrma* (for blinking), *krikala* (for gastric secretion), *devadatta* (for yawning) and *dhananjaya* (for distributing nourishment).

Viveka. Discrimination.

Perception of the distinction between the self or pure consciousness and that picture of himself which each person makes.

Is helped by a seven-fold understanding, having reference to separation of the Looker-on from four bodily and three mental conditions (pain, pleasure, liking or desire, disliking or aversion, thought, feeling and the will).

Vrikshāsana.
(The Tree Posture)

Stand on one leg; bend the other leg at the knee so that the foot rests high up on the thigh of the straight leg.

Vrittis. (Literally whirlpools).

The *vrittis* (ideas) in the lower mind (*chitta*) are given by Patanjali as occurring in five groups: (1) correct ideas, (2) wrong ideas, (3) fancies, (4) ideas obtained during sleep, and (5) memories.

These five are respectively named in Sanskrit *pramana, viparyaya, vikalpa, midrā,* and *smriti.*

It is important that whenever an idea rises before the mind it should *instantly* be recognized as belonging to one or other of these five classes. If this function fails the person will be insane. To classify our ideas in this respect correctly as they come up, instantly and instinctively, is the sign of a healthy mind. Ideas, as materials for thinking with, must be controlled. Thinking is, in fact, the marshalling of ideas which themselves must be definite and unchanging. Ideas are further classified as painful or pleasant in all cases.

Vyāhritis.

The three introductory words

recited, after *Om,* at the beginning of the *Gāyatrī Mantra (q.v.).* They are mystical utterances, but at the same time they remind the reciter of the three *lokas* (q.v.) or regions in which a similtaneous effect of the prayer is desired. They are named *bhū, bhuva, swar.*

Vyāna.

That *Vital Air (q.v.)* which is described as carrying all over the body something that is essential in all the channels. It must have some particular relation also to the *chakra* between the basal and the navel (see *Swādhisthāna Chakra),* connected with the prostatic plexus, and there is logic in this, since excessive sexual activity or even the thought of it, appears to deplete the general vitality of the whole body, while on the other hand the conservation of sexual forces tends to the greater vitality of the body for all purposes. The statement of the yogīs with regard to this matter goes much further, and affirms that when there is continence in thought and deed this vital air ascends the spinal channel and greatly energizes the high centres connected with the higher mind and spiritual intuition.

The color of this *vāyu* seems to be red, rosy, pale rose or "as of a ray of light." This is no doubt what is usually called the general health aura, seen extending a little outside the body, and as appearing sturdy when there is good health and feeble and droopy when the health is poor. There is some taking and giving in this matter, so that contacts with other persons definitely affect our vitality for good or ill. Also when there is abundance of this aura it can be deliberately given or sent to others who need it.

Vyāsa.

Famous classical commentator on the Yoga-sūtras of Patanjali.

W

Waking State, The.
(See under Avasthās).

Wall-gazing.

A method of meditation among the Zen Buddhists, in which the yogī sits looking "like a wall"—not looking *at* a wall, as some have mistakenly thought—that is, without any desire, interest or intention.

Wisdom.
(See under Buddhi).

World, the; or, What is Seen.
(drishya).

It consists of objects and senses. It is understandable, is moving and unmoving, and has the three *gunas (q.v.)*. It is useful for experience and fulfillment or liberation, and in fact exists for the sake of the Looker-on. Its forms are made by karmas due to *kleshas (q.v.)*, and cease for a given man when these cease, there being, for each, "my world," his game in the hall of many games.

Worlds, The Three.

This expression usually refers to the regions of our body, our emotions (sometimes called *kāma-loka*) and our lower or concrete minds. All three are regarded as objective planes or levels, the first having forms produced by actions, the second by emotions, the third by thoughts. When released from the ballast of the body and the stimulus of environment during sleep most people are quite incoherent, lacking in concentration and in consecutive thought, in the *kāmic* and mental regions, but some are wide awake, active and purposeful, even though they may not be able to remember this part of their lives when they are awake in the body.

Y

Yajna. (Sacrifice, q.v.).

Yājnavalkya.

Famous rishi or seer of ancient India, spoken about in the *Brihadāranyaka Upanishad*, who lived over 3,000 years ago, and taught philosophy and yoga, notably the doctrine that everything exists for the Self *(Ātmā)* which he explained to his wife Maitreyī.

Yajnopavīta. (Sacred thread.)

The triple thread worn by Brahmins *(q.v.)* — those who are dedicated to Brahman. When the thread is newly worn the following words are spoken: "Put on the *yajnopavīta,* the supreme, the holy, which came into existence along with the *Prajāpati* (father of all creatures), which gives long life and is very excellent. Let this give you strength and light." This triple thread is a symbol or reminder of the triple Brahman. The yogī, however, discards it, as he now knows that he has in himself the indestructible supreme Brahman. He wears that within.

Yoga.

Literally union. The state of a man when his life of action and thought is entirely in harmony with the very source or root of his being.

There are varieties of yoga, such as the yogas of action *(karma)*, worship *(bhakti)*, and knowledge *(jnāna* or *gnyāna)*, and yoga with the aid of ordered breathings and postures *(hatha-yoga)*, the raising of the spinal forces *(laya-yoga)*, the use of effective recitations *(mantra-yoga)*, and yoga by means of meditation and contemplation *(rāja-yoga)*.

It is implicit that this union and the practices being done to achieve it are always voluntary and conscious, never passive.

It is very important to realize that the high achievements of yoga are going to be attained *without knowing how*. The how is for the smaller and preparatory matters. Man has in himself great potentialities for unfoldment, when he tries. All this is analogous to the way in which a child learns to walk without knowing how.

Union with the divine is the ultimate aim, but in the meantime the term is used relatively, so there can be union with knowledge *(jnāna-yoga)*, union with wisdom *(buddhi-yoga)*, union with the true self *(ātmā-yoga)*. There is also a distinction of method, as in union by control or power *(rāja-yoga— rāja* meaning king)*, union by devotion *(bhakti-yoga)*, union by science *(sānkhya-yoga)*, union by incantations *(mantra-yoga)*, etc.

Yoga Philosophy.

The yoga philosophy is spiritual; it aims at the individual discovery and realization in consciousness of the independent, self-existing, self-originating spirit *(purusha)* of man. It is ethical; the system of eight steps or limbs starts with five virtues, of which noninjury is the first. It is intellectual; its methods of meditation are applications of the powers of the mind, and its philosophy gives reasons for all its aphorisms. It is emotional; it prescribes friendliness, sympathy and other good feelings. It is practical; it deals with the government and regulation of the body by the man within. There are many different schools and teachers, emphasizing different parts of the teaching, but all look back to Patanjali *(q.v.)* as the great and respected codifier of the *rāja-yoga* system.

Yogārūdha.

A term describing one who is well established in yoga practice. *Ārūdha* means "mounted," as when one mounts a horse.

Yogī or yogin.

One who practices yoga. Feminine: yoginī.

Z

Zen.

A system of mental stillness, employed for the attainment of complete release from attachment to the objective world. The word *zen* is a modification of the Sanskrit word for meditation *(dhyāna)*, which became *chan* in China and *Zen* in Japan. It depends largely upon three methods of stopping the flow of mentality, by means of wall-gazing, the *mondo* *(q.v.)* and the *koan (q.v.)* which then permit an experience by direct perception (or intuition) which is called a *satori*.

Meditation in the *zen* system can be described as "seeing without desire," and the height of it is reached when there is direct perception and the stoppage of reasoning. It involves "Drop it" as far as thought is concerned, but "Go on" as far as consciousness is concerned. This is not essentially different from the original Hindu idea on the subject, which is that the inner light of the mind will be found to be shining when external desires pass away.